Slum Acts

After the Postcolonial
A series sponsored by the Smuts Memorial Fund
University of Cambridge

AbdouMaliq Simone, *Improvised Lives*
Veena Das, *Slum Acts*

Slum Acts

Veena Das

polity

Copyright © Veena Das 2022

The right of Veena Das to be identified as Author of this Work has been asserted in accordance with the UK Copyright, Designs and Patents Act 1988.

First published in 2022 by Polity Press

Polity Press
65 Bridge Street
Cambridge CB2 1UR, UK

Polity Press
101 Station Landing
Suite 300
Medford, MA 02155, USA

All rights reserved. Except for the quotation of short passages for the purpose of criticism and review, no part of this publication may be reproduced, stored in a retrieval system or transmitted, in any form or by any means, electronic, mechanical, photocopying, recording or otherwise, without the prior permission of the publisher.

ISBN-13: 978-1-5095-3785-3
ISBN-13: 978-1-5095-3786-0 (pb)

A catalogue record for this book is available from the British Library.

Library of Congress Control Number: 2021942993

Typeset in 11 on 13pt Sabon LT Pro
by Cheshire Typesetting Ltd, Cuddington, Cheshire
Printed and bound in Great Britain by TJ Books Ltd, Padstow, Cornwall

The publisher has used its best endeavours to ensure that the URLs for external websites referred to in this book are correct and active at the time of going to press. However, the publisher has no responsibility for the websites and can make no guarantee that a site will remain live or that the content is or will remain appropriate.

Every effort has been made to trace all copyright holders, but if any have been overlooked the publisher will be pleased to include any necessary credits in any subsequent reprint or edition.

For further information on Polity, visit our website:
politybooks.com

Contents

v

Acknowledgments

I was privileged to be invited to deliver the Smuts Lectures at the University of Cambridge in 2018 and want to thank Professors Ash Amin, Sruti Kapila, and Saul Debow for this invitation and the intellectual stimulation they provided during my visit. Professor Amin graciously steered discussions during the public lectures and seminars, creating an environment of intellectual excitement and vibrant exchange of ideas. I want to thank particularly James Laidlaw, Marilyn Strathern, Caroline Humphrey, Joel Robbins, Heonik Kwon, Perveez Mody, and David Mosse for their critical attention to the details that allow concepts to emerge within the ethnography.

Over the years, I have learnt much from discussions with Clara Han, Nayanika Mookherjee, Bhrigupati Singh, Sruti Chaganti, Pooja Satyogi, Aditi Saraf, Megha Sehdev, Kunal Joshi, Vaibhav Saria, Anna Wherry, Pratiksha Baxi, Didier Fassin, and Naveeda Khan on matters relating to law, policing, and surveillance. During the period of intense isolation and repeated illnesses of the COVID year that I lived through, I was

Acknowledgments

privileged to count on Andrew Brandel, Michael Puett, Lotte Segal, and Nayan Das to be with me to form a protective circle that sustained thought through words and gestures of care. With what words can I thank my friends Deepak Mehta, Rita Brara, Pratiksha Baxi, and Roma Chatterji? Roma allowed me access to a trunkful of court documents she had collected but was not planning to work with; and Deepak, Pratiksha, and Rita shared insights on events for which I could not be present in Delhi. My family members, from the oldest to the youngest, have astonishing abilities to be supportive and critical at the same time – so, thank you guys for not giving up on me. I also want to thank the doctors, nurses, and staff of Ellison 10 at Mass General Hospital for their outstanding teamwork, expertise, and care; and my gratitude goes to Drs. Das, Iyasere, and Simmone for guiding me toward recovery.

I gratefully acknowledge the kindness of Professor John Thompson, Neil de Cort and Julia Davies at Polity Press, and Professor Amin once again, in steering the book toward completion. Thanks to Ian Tuttle for excellent copy-editing. I wish David Held had been there for continuing our conversations along with Eva-Maria Nag, and Nayanika Mookherjee at Durham. I so miss not being able to share this work with David.

I want to thank the two anonymous reviewers whose comments were incredibly helpful in making revisions to the book at a time when I was not able to see my way through the difficulties this material presented. I am more grateful than I can say to the residents of the neighborhoods in Delhi where I have worked for sharing their lives with me and my colleagues at the Institute for Socio-Economic Research on Development and Democracy (ISERDD).

This book is dedicated to Abdul Wahid Shaikh, whose courage, integrity, and intellectual provocations to make thought count make it a privilege to be able to claim him as a friend.

Veena Das
Baltimore, July 2021

I
Introduction

Slum Acts is written in these ominous times when the surveillance apparatus of the state in India is being used to curb all dissent, accompanied by a draconian curbing of political liberties and dismantling of the research infrastructure that once allowed the social sciences to flourish in India. Simultaneously, global theories of violence, civil war, terrorism, torture, or policing demonstrate the increasing influence of the security apparatus of the state on academic writing (Whitehead 2012). A global discourse on the threat of international terrorism has allowed reputed scholars to defend the use of torture by the evocation of scenarios of extreme emergency and, while much discussion has focused on the brutality of civil wars waged by non-state actors, the role of states as collaborators of these non-state actors, as financiers of the weapons used in civil wars, or the direct violence perpetrated at a distance by states through drone attacks, carpet bombing, or torture in offshore prisons, is made to disappear. This book takes on the problematic of the violence perpetrated through the security apparatus of the state and its relation to judicial logic applied in both states of emergency as well as in the hurly-burly of everyday urban life. The close relation between policing and urban existence was of much interest to Foucault (2008) but while he was looking at police ordinances and absorption of disbanded solders at the end of war, *Slum Acts* asks how the imagination of slums as specific sites of urban disorder comes to be connected with the imaginary of transnational terrorism. And though from a distance it might seem that judicial logic in the case of regulation of urban populations might be very different from the judicial logic in the case of terror trials, we find surprising resonances between the two. This is not to say that the specter of terrorist violence does not produce an intensification of cruel practices in the way police investigate terror-related cases but that there is no sharp dividing line between the two.

I do not start with a set of ready-made concepts which I can simply apply to the questions that animate this book, but perhaps I can say how my questions developed as a result of a long-term ethnography of what I call urban slums here as a short-hand term, but which can include many different categories of spaces defined primarily through their relation to the classifying and regulating mechanisms of urban governance. (For my work on these localities, see especially Das 2011, 2014, 2020; Das & Walton 2015.) I will introduce these areas, briefly commenting on my use of the term slum, but first, let me lay out the questions I explore.

First, I in am interested in asking how to understand the temporality of a catastrophic event such as a series of terrorist attacks on a city. In media representations and in one reading of the judicial process, what follows a terrorist attack is a series of linear actions – the event, its investigation, court trial, and fixing of responsibility, followed by sentencing and punishment. This particular idea of the event, as bounded and occurring in a linear succession of actions, often obscures from view the actual bundling of smaller events which cluster together and radiate in different directions, such as identifying suspects, interrogations, production of police documents, witness statements, court hearings, postponements, compromises; I argue that it is in these details that one can find the way something like a terror-related investigation spreads its tentacles into communities from which suspects are picked up, relatives and friends are forced to give testimonies against them, and whole communities are stigmatized and rendered guilty by association. Further, I ask, how are cruel and inhuman punishments, including torture, absorbed into the life of communities? I examine the relation between subjugated knowledges and what I call "inordinate knowledge" to retrieve and take forward the writings of a torture survivor, Abdul Wahid Shaikh, to claim for his incredible writing the status of social theory that undoes the plethora of justifications for torture that have been crafted by learned jurists and professors.

Second, I ask how does the fact that the police as a biopolitical body is dispersed in the neighborhoods that comprise these slums affect the texture of relations as neighbors come to suspect that some among them are police informers, or that policemen posted in the *chaukis* (outposts), presumably to prevent crime, are, in fact, working with the land mafias or traffickers? In what way may we then think of the relation between the rogue power exercised by the police and the judicial process? How does one study the decentered or dispersed processes though which judicial truth is constituted? Are fictions of the law opposed to its truth or are they truth's doubles?

Third, how does anthropology channel the expressions that are produced within neighborhoods steeped in the ever-present potential for violence (Motta 2020) without falling into statist definitions of what is terror, or guilt? Above all I want to understand how life is remade, not through any grand gestures of forgiveness and reconciliation, but through an ethics and aesthetics of the everyday. Being able to grasp that the inhuman forms of cruelty I saw or felt, were, after all, not the work of monsters but an eventuality in the career of the human, was an idea I could understand in the abstract. But seeing this connection in the concrete lives of human beings with bodies and names was one of the greatest difficulties of reality I experienced. It marks every word I speak about them and the milieu in which perpetrators of such cruel acts and their victims continue to inhabit the same social spaces. Sometimes one says disparagingly that one could do nothing else but push on. But I came to realize, yet once again, that life can only be knitted together pair by pair (see Cavell 2007b). This book is a further step into these vexed issues.

Let me first introduce some of the features of the slums that have direct implications for understanding what transpires in the next three chapters.

Slum Actions and Definitions

Much of the recent literature on slums sees them as directly connected to the growth of megacities in the Global South. As peripheries to these megacities, the slums are seen as both steeped in crime and squalor and essential for the kinds of services they provide to the residents of more affluent areas. In many ways, these theories build on Simmel's (1965) understanding of the poor as defined not only by material deprivation but by the kinds of sociality that defines them (see Das and Randeria 2015).

4

Writing from the perspective of subaltern studies, some theorists have proposed theorizing slums as spaces of habitation, livelihood, self-organization, and politics rather than spaces of material deprivation and political disorder (see V. Rao 2006; Roy 2011; Simone 2004, 2019). Many activists and others working in these areas rightly protest against the picture of urban disorder located within slums and object to the use of the word "slum" for its derogatory implications. In addition to flourishing economic enterprises in these areas, they say, life in slums has evolved its own norms and its own norm-producing mechanisms that are not dependent on the state. For example, they point to informal arrangements such as rights established over what is known as *kabza* land (occupied land), or the negotiations with employees of electricity companies such as linemen working on the ground to reduce costs of electricity, and so on. Yet, what gets elided in these descriptions is first, the sheer heterogeneity within and among slum populations in terms of access to economic resources; and second, the penetration of state agencies into the everyday life of inhabitants living in these areas.

Consider, the flourishing enterprises in places like Dharavi, regarded as the biggest slum in Asia. These enterprises are evidence of the ability to innovate and the organizational skills of the people residing there. But their prosperity is also built on the fact that owners of these enterprises who live and work in Dharavi are able to extract cheap labor from less fortunate kin or new migrants who use their networks to come to the city and hence start by being dependent on these networks. Over time, these kin or these migrants may be able to make a better life for themselves or not, but the success stories of some are built on the misery of others who might well accept these deprivations in hopes for better futures.

Second, the emphasis on informality overlooks the fact that the success of informal arrangements is also dependent on legal or bureaucratic provisions that were successfully adjudicated in some cases but not in others. Elsewhere, I have analyzed two different court cases and their afterlives in two such neighborhoods in Delhi. In one case residents successfully petitioned the High Court and obtained a stay order against eviction from their shanties. At the same time, the court also ordered surveys of all households to determine who could claim alternate accommodations that it held the government was obliged to provide to eligible residents of the area. It turned out to be impossible for the local-level bureaucrats to complete this task within the stipulated time, which generated more court cases, with the result that people could not be evicted but neither could the promise of alternative housing be realized. (The situation, as people often pointed out to me, was radically different in Dharavi where in many cases builders directly negotiated with slum dwellers to get land vacated by offering them alternate housing.)

In the court case in the second locality, where residents were fighting a powerful educational society who claimed original rights over land they had occupied, cooperation between the local branch of a political party and a nongovernmental organization (NGO) were successful in thwarting the case in court (see Das and Walton 2015). My point is that though the different categories of urban spaces identified by official administrative bodies are a mishmash of different kinds of categories, these official categories have consequences. As Subbaraman et al. (2015) showed, for instance, health outcomes for residents of notified slums in Mumbai are decisively better than the health outcomes for residents of non-notified slums.[1] The formal/informal divide does little work here as it completely obliterates from view the hard work slum dwellers do to engage the formal institutions such as courts of law to sustain their lives; nor does this divide work when the apparatus of the state is visible and tangible in every nook and cranny of these slums and settlements. Rather, the task is to see the complex interplay between affordances and constraints; between the fine lattice of formal and informal institutions, and the tensions and alliance among them. Certainly, the residents of these localities can find moments of ecstasy in performing dances or songs with visiting dignitaries, and organize themselves during elections or go to protest marches, and all of these are important forms of political actions. Yet, they can be left with little recourse when embroiled falsely in court cases under terror-related legislation, or tortured in prison, or discover that a child was abducted by a neighbor and trafficked but the police refuse to register even a First Information Report (FIR) to begin investigations.

The searing questions we might ask, then, are questions like, why is torture practiced in a democracy, why does it take weeks to get an FIR registered when my child fails to return home, how can we live with the knowledge that we gave false evidence under pressure from the police? These questions lead to new provocations for social theory of which I identify three specific issues: (a) the distinction between so-called civilized and barbaric violence; (b) locating alternate genealogies for theories of sovereignty; and (c) inordinate knowledge.

Violence: Civilized vs. Savage

In the opening lines of this *Introduction*, I stated that that there is an increasing resonance between academic writing and statist logic. This is not a novel argument: Deleuze and Guattari (1987), as also Foucault (1990), observed the close ties between what is imagined as the destiny of the state and the destiny of thinking. As Deleuze and Guattari wrote:

> There exists a Hegelianism of the right that lives on in official political philosophy and weds the destiny of thought to the State ... From Hegel to Max Weber there developed a whole line of reflection of the relation of the modern State to Reason, both as rational-technical and as reasonable-human. If it is objected that this rationality, already present in the archaic imperial State, is the *optimum* of the governors themselves, the Hegelians respond that the rational-reasonable cannot exist without a minimum of participation of everybody. The question, rather, is whether the very form of rational-reasonable is not extracted from the State, in a way that necessarily makes it right, gives it "reason." (p. 556, n. 42)

How does the unspoken alliance between state discourses on where threats to safety and security lie and academic writing structure thought so as to render such practices as torture and coercive interrogation techniques thinkable within liberal democracies (Ahmad and Lilienthal 2016)? Talal Asad has argued that the September 11 attacks in New York initiated a revival of interest in just war theory not only because the US imagined a new kind of war to have been initiated by these attacks (the "War on Terror"), but also because of the pressures in liberal democracies to distinguish their own acts of violence, characterized as rational and bounded, versus the violence of the terrorists, seen as driven by passion and, therefore, excessive and indiscriminate (Asad 2010; see also the stringent critique of Hegelian thinking in relation to colonialism in Guha 2002).

I will not rehearse here the many contradictions that Asad systematically demonstrates in just war theory or the subtle changes that creep into this theory when compared with its theological origins pertaining to ideas of fairness and justice in war. What I want to suggest is that there was a ready-made theoretical apparatus available in the distinction between civilized violence of state-initiated wars and barbaric violence attributed to others, whether colonial subjects or Islamic fighters, who were seen as outside this apparatus that supposedly used violence as bounded by rationality and ethics. This opposition helps decipher how one might explain the most horrific acts of destruction on the part of Western countries to have been considered just, because they were driven by a principle – the principle of proportionate harm. This is how an equation was made between the Japanese who died as a result of the bombing of Hiroshima and Nagasaki and the number of Allied deaths during World War II through the techniques of warfare used by both parties to the war. The hollowness of these principles is stunning, but the fact that those responsible for the dropping of the atom bomb could escape any charges of war crimes is partly because the victor sets the rules for what will be counted against what. As Kennedy (2006) so aptly puts it:

> Putting ourselves back in the legitimate position of Truman's wartime decision making, we ask: how many allied soldiers were saved by the bomb? Not Japanese civilians or soldiers but Allied soldiers against Japanese bomb deaths. Estimates differ. In June 1945, the Joint Chiefs estimated 40,000. In 1945 Truman said he had estimated 250,000. In his memoirs, written ten years after the fact, Truman used the figure 500,000. Churchill, in 1953, estimated a million Americans and 500,000 British troops. In 1991, President Bush claimed the use of atomic bombs had "spared millions of American lives." (p. 146)

If the principle of proportionality was used to explain the "justness" of the dropping of atomic bombs on Hiroshima and Nagasaki, the discourse on the war on terrorism does not compare in numbers. For instance, justifications offered for war on cities (that includes bombing areas where civilians reside, including hospitals and schools), as by Israel, are not based on comparison of numbers but on the irrationality of the techniques used by terrorists. The claim in such cases is that it is not a question of how many died in a terror attack, but of terror spread in whole populations, but completely ignoring the terror of bombs raining down from the sky. This discourse on the violence of non-state actors then reinstitutes the dividing line between civilized, rational violence and barbaric, indiscriminate violence. So firmly is the idea that the civilizing processes in Europe under modernity led to constraints on indiscriminate violence engrained in theories of war, that even those who question the "explanations" of why civil wars are more brutal than wars waged by states, do not ask if the question itself is correctly posed. Thus, for instance, Kalyvas (2006), in his comprehensive study on the logic of violence in civil war, starts his chapter on barbarism with the statement: "Despite a quasi-universal recognition of an association between civil war and atrocity, there is surprising[ly] little in the way of specified links between the two" (p. 52). He recognizes the absurdity of the presumption that killing with machetes is less civilized than killing with bullets or bombs, yet somehow continues to support the notion that European countries were more successful in making a sharp division between combatants and civilians, the widespread use of torture and rape to "pacify" populations in colonial wars notwithstanding. Nor does he question whether the role played by European countries in developing technologies of torture, such as France's contribution to so-called "clean torture" with electricity, did not indicate pathologies of civilization.[2]

I argue that the emergence of discussions as to whether an extreme emergency created by international terrorism justifies use of torture in public discussions not only elides the violence perpetrated by Western democracies in their colonial and neocolonial projects, but is also heavily dependent on the use of counterfactuals, scenario building, thought experiments, analogies, and narrative tropes that end up dressing a subjunctive, as-if model or scenario such as the ticking bomb scenario, into the language of actuality. It is not that the empirical is totally lacking in these discussions, but the large data sets gathered on types of conflict, their intensity or duration, reflect essentially statist interests through which such practices as torture can be defended as regrettable, but necessary. Further, modes of surveillance can be extended to cover those segments of the population defined as "vulnerable" to propaganda emerging from extremist projects, and hence potentially dangerous for the security of the nation state. For instance, the discourse of preventing young Muslims from "becoming radicalized" is an important component on policy making in many countries including the UK, but interestingly excludes those who might be radicalized by racist ideologies of white supremacy, and extreme emergencies focus on foreign terrorists but do not include such violence as repeated instances of gun violence against schoolchildren in the US.[3]

This book confronts these boundary-making discourses between state and non-state actors, rational violence of the state as opposed to the irrational violence of non-state actors (including terrorists) at several levels. First, it tries to dismantle the assumed ground-figure relation that takes for granted that sites for observing the apparatus of state are naturally courts of law, police stations, police patrols, or offices of bureaucrats. Strategies of research based on this ground-figure relation settle on spatial imageries that conceptualize power through location rather than circulation, rendering matters of scale in terms of containment of smaller units into larger ones.

I propose, instead, to think of scale through a dynamic relation between parts and wholes – each might be reconstituted standing in a dynamic relation to each other. After all, we know that from some perspectives a part can be larger than the whole because in taking its place among other parts, any one part is likely to lose some of its distinctive attributes that were manifested when it stood alone. Thus, when I track the manner in which the police posts function in the slums of Delhi or Mumbai, certain aspects of the mechanisms of govern-ance are revealed that are not apparent in such sites as a court of law where a judge is rearranging the facts, in the process of a criminal hearing as lawyers and witnesses are made to recount events in an adversarial setting. In fact, neither objects implicated in a crime, nor subjects remain stable as they move from one place to another, say from a neighborhood in which a fight occurred to the police station or a court of law: nor is the order of recounting an event in everyday life in the slums of the same order as recounting the same event in a court under the pressure of legal definitions of relevance, direct witnessing, hearsay, and cross-examination.[4] In other words, the story of a crime and of policing that one elicits through ongoing participation in the life of a slum might remain in the confines of this local milieu or it might move along different networks that draw upon NGOs, politicians, policemen, and become grafted onto other events, ending up in a court of law. However, we cannot simply add up the different components of these stories as if these were pieces of a jigsaw puzzle that will "naturally" fit into a pattern. Instead, we might think of a fragment as it breaks from one context and attaches itself to another one in ways that its earlier location might be made to disappear or the fragment might disturb the harmony of its new location (see Das 2007, 2020).

In a recent paper, Kublitz (2021) offers a fine example of marrying scale to perspective as she tracks the killing by the Danish police force of a petty criminal, called Omar, whose Muslim identity leads the police to remake the narrative of his killing by elevating his actions and attributing them to the actions of a "foreign terrorist." What is interesting in Kublitz's analysis is that she shows how simultaneously his life within the local-level gang-related violence is engulfed and made to disappear as the narrative of the foreign terrorist takes hold of public imagination and in the strategic reasoning of security forces. We can see that the more global story of Western countries under threat from Islamic terrorism does not so much contain the history of police actions and inactions at the lower level, as make them irrelevant for the more globally recognizable story and subsequent investment of vast resources in the industry of policing projects to combat radicalization of Muslim youth. As we will see in the next chapter, those who are attentive judges in the courts in India set up to investigate terror-related crimes always consider the possibility that the police are trying to solve the problem of gang-related violence by pushing the case as a terror-related case so as to avoid normal legal procedures.

The picture of parts that fit into coherent wholes is precisely what gives power to statist knowledge because the discordance and disharmony that would result from a mereological form of reasoning is made to disappear by the assumption that the whole by definition includes the parts, and that what is true for the encompassing whole (e.g., the state) must be true for each of its constituent parts (e.g., communities, families), since these parts stand in a nested relation where larger parts contain the smaller ones. As we shall see, this kind of formulation makes the specificity of local events disappear as generalizations are generated to tell "the bigger story." This formulation invites a consideration of the possibility of alternate genealogies of sovereignty than within the statist ideology we located in the boundaries drawn between civilized and barbaric violence.

Sovereignty: Alternate Genealogies

The distinguished anthropologist and crusader for peace, Alex de Waal, who has studied the political processes of civil war and failure of international peacemaking pacts in Darfur over more than 25 years, argues that when we shift attention from theories of sovereignty that rest on assumptions of the state's capacity to enforce order, to the domain of real politics, what we encounter is a marketplace of disorderly transactions at every level of the political system (de Waal 2015, 2021). For some other scholars, the conflation of authority and power on the side of the state signals an erosion of the authority of the people and the subsequent rise of populism and its right-wing manifestations (Bargu 2021). A puzzle remains though, for, as Lemaitre (2021) asks, how do we explain the faith people put in the law to put limits on violence, when decades of experience in the postcolony has shown that much violence actually resides within the law? De Waal writes from his experience of participation in peacemaking efforts and his ethnography of negotiations among high officials; Lemaitre writes as a lawyer and now judge in Colombia who has participated in activist projects with displaced women over a number of years. These experiences have given these scholars an acute sense of the contradictions within the law and a deep distrust of very neat theories of sovereignty.

As with these scholars, my own interest in alternate

genealogies of sovereignty does not arise so much from abstract theorizing as from trying to make sense of the grains of experience in which these contradictory impulses toward the whole apparatus of the state were visible and tangible in the lives of people in the slums. I turn to Georges Dumézil, the scholar of Indo-European mythology, and his formulations on sovereignty, not because he provides some kind of master key to understand sovereignty but because the mythological register in his work allows different aspects of sovereignty to emerge. I might add in parentheses that a number of my interlocutors would evoke mythological figures, including Rama, Krishna and some minor figures from the Mahabharata or from contemporary renderings of these figures in films, to make a point during a discussion. I don't dwell much on this strand of my ethnography in the following analysis but it gives me some confidence in making my arguments through the use of mythological figures (see especially Singh 2015).

There is a large and impressive literature pertaining to Dumézil's notions of sovereignty but, with rare exceptions, it has not been mobilized to think of the character of the modern state – most of the discussion is confined to scholarly circles within Indo-European studies. I am not claiming that it is easy to make Vedic gods speak to contemporary concerns but texts surely have not only a past but also a future if their potential can be marshalled with them and even against them. It is in this spirit that I offer the discussion on the double-headed character of sovereignty, symbolized by the Vedic Gods, Mitra and Varuna – the former standing for the pact-making aspects of sovereignty (pacts include contracts that are both legal and clandestine); and the latter standing for force exercised within the logic of sovereignty. Outside these two poles is the war machine personified in the warrior god Indra, whose functions cannot be absorbed within the double-headed sovereignty and is exterior to the state apparatus.

In their book, *A thousand plateaus*, Gilles Deleuze and Félix Guattari (1987) make an interesting intervention through Dumézil's text on Mitra-Varuna, drawing attention to the fact that sovereignty includes the despot *and* the legislator; the fearsome and the regulated; the bond and the pact. But there is something in sovereignty, they say, that exceeds the Mitra-Varuna function, in that the Indra function stands for notions of unlimited cruelty and unlimited compassion, violence and justice, that are imagined outside the apparatus of the state. I don't stand by every strand of interpretation of the Mitra-Varuna functions in either Dumézil or in Deleuze and Guattari, but that they open certain doors for thinking of sovereignty outside the political theories inherited from Christian theology is not in question for me. I will indicate some of the difficulties when it comes to the specificity of these Vedic gods or their relation to the characters in the Mahabharata on whom Dumézil later tries to map these functions. For now, I am interested in the way these ideas on sovereignty have been absorbed in the work of some anthropologists.

Bhrigupati Singh (2012) takes the figures of Varuna and Mitra and demonstrates how they become productive figures of thought to illuminate his rich ethnography of the State in rural Rajasthan. In addition to showing how the twin figures of Mitra-Varuna function in connection with the people's encounters with state-level bureaucrats, Singh's discussion includes a substantive discussion of the demotion of Indra in Indian mythology. There are some beautiful moments in the text, where he shows how traces of mythological stories pertaining to Indra continue to animate conversations on, for instance, the sin Indra committed in seducing the wife of the sage Gautam, or his defeat at the hands of the child Krishna. The problem of the warrior, Singh says, citing Dumézil, is that, "Theologically and possibly socially the most difficult task had to be carried out against the traditional warriors, human and divine; the problem was to redeploy them in the service of the good religion, to preserve their force while depriving them of their autonomy" (cited in Singh 2015: 176). In tracking the various ways mythological elements are rearranged in oral epics and in everyday conversations in his field site, Singh wants to capture the dynamism of local deities through new versions of the hero function. It remains unclear, however, whether, unlike the Mitra-Varuna functions which Singh finds in the actual interactions of people with the state functionaries, the Indra version remains at the level of mythology and folklore; or, if there are other regions of life in Shahbad in which resonances to the sins of the warrior are to be found.

Chaganti (2020) is interested in the figure of Indra for a different reason. Working in the courts in Karnataka and following court cases inside the court and in the offices of the lawyers, she wants to capture the rogue element of sovereignty that works both inside and outside the law even as judges and lawyers are engaged in formal hearings as well as in deal making in the corridors of the courts, parliaments, or in smoky cafés. I think Chaganti is right in thinking that a rogue element characterizes the kind of sovereignty Indra embodies. Indra commits, at different times, every sin that Dumézil thinks the warrior is prone to commit and on each occasion one of his powers leaves and goes to some other God. But Chaganti's ethnography shows that, far from succeeding in taking the warrior god and redeploying him in the service of the good religion, the rogue function gets absorbed within sovereignty.[5] In my understanding the rogue element of sovereignty is what suddenly, without warning, upends the pact-making aspects that people might have put together through a tacit understanding of the pairing of force with contract.

All these components of Dumézil's formulation on the Vedic gods as figures of thought on sovereignty serve very well to complicate sovereignty beyond the notion of the sovereign having the right to declare the exception, but what if we were to take the gaps and puzzles that remain if we were to delve deeper into the relation between the Vedic gods and the resonances with the stories of the Mahabharata on which Dumézil drew famously to formulate his theory of the tripartite division of functions?[6] Nicholas Allen (1999) has argued for a functional equivalence between Indra and Arjun (in the Mahabharata) since both stand for the warrior function, but one could very well argue that it is Krishna who is the real agent of the war and is recognized as such by Gandhari, the mother of the Kaurava brothers, when she curses Krishna for having enabled the war to happen in which all her sons perish?[7] Second, and from my point of view, an even greater difficulty arises when we consider the goddess figures (particularly war goddesses, or goddesses of fire) in the Indo-Aryan pantheon. Dumézil was inclined to think of the trivalent heroine or the goddess as coming either from the second, warrior function, or from the third function of fertility and prosperity. However, given the difficulties of assigning gender to some Indo-Aryan figures of divinity and the propensity of goddesses to disguise themselves with male names, it would seem that the relation between sovereignty and sexuality needs considerable work if alternate genealogies of sovereignty are to be developed further.[8]

Finally, in his extraordinary work on temple deities in Jaffna during the period this territory was under the control of the militant LTTE (Tamil Tigers) that waged a war against the State in Sri Lanka (see Spencer 2002), Sidharthan Maunaguru (2020) proposes to think of the vulnerability of sovereignty. Even at the height of its power, he says, the LTTE could not take control over the temples, which retained a measure of autonomy from the LTTE. Maunaguru suggests that one thing which the mythology of gods and goddesses in Hinduism teaches us is that even at the height of their powers, these deities are compelled to share power with other deities, such as folk deities. This formulation should alert us to the fact that, unlike the singular God of Semitic traditions, the deities in the Rigveda appear in groups and are highly volatile. There is, for instance, only one hymn dedicated exclusively to Mitra. Mitra himself might be interpreted as a god who presides over contracts, or alliances, or over the morning light. And in fact, in order to be manifested in the morning so that the darkness of the night might be dispelled, he depends on Agni (fire), the deity who knows the Vedas in their entirety to be ignited, but the Mitra function of pact-making here is not seen as twinned with the Varuna function of force. If notions of sovereignty underlying modern States are to be regarded as secularized theological concepts, then these works encourage us to think of other theologies to provide different pathways to the problem of sovereignty in contemporary contexts.

I leave this as a marker of work to come, but I am convinced that we could tell the story of sovereignty and state by drawing on the potential of these stories just as Singh's interlocutors do when they redistribute the different mythological elements in new configurations.

Knowledge That Wounds

In the two previous sections I looked at different ways knowledge was inflected with statist interests. Foucault

(2003, 2006) famously evoked the figure of the grotesque to describe such disciplinary knowledge in which tokens of power come to stand for disciplinary authority. His corpus of work has been marshalled to suggest contestation, resistance, or struggle, as a counter to such expert knowledge. I do not underestimate the importance of being able to tell "counter-stories" or to make subjugated knowledge appear in the light of critique that is grounded in the experiences that these stories tell (Torre et al. 2001). Yet I want to touch on another register of the darkness of knowledge that is carried, endured, and worked on in the everyday.

In proposing the concept of inordinate knowledge, I readily concede that it remains to be fully developed in the philosophical and anthropological literature; yet, I find that even if some aspects of this concept remain obscure to me, I find it to be powerful in the way it goes beyond the issue of specific speech acts to that of our experience of language as a whole. The concept first emerged in an essay by Stanley Cavell (2007a) which grew into earlier and later versions (in 2007 and 2010) he wrote in conversation with Cora Diamond in response to what she called "the difficulty of reality" and the "difficulty of philosophy" (Diamond 2008, earlier version 2003). In his essay Cavell characterized the sense of woundedness that Diamond gave expression to as "inordinate knowledge," attaching a string of attributes, not so much to define this concept as to convey its feel.[9] For Cavell, inordinate knowledge may be characterized as knowledge that can seem "excessive in its expression, in contrast to mere or bare or pale or intellectualized or uninsistent or inattentive or distracted or filed, archived knowledge, an opposite direction of questionable, here defective, or insipid, or shallow, or indecisive expression" (Cavell 2010: 84). In order to flesh out this concept and to indicate its salience for me,

I will dwell in some detail on the conversation between Cavell and Diamond and then give some examples from my ethnography to say what I hope in absorbing this idea into anthropological modes of description or analysis.

In the citation from Cavell I gave, he makes a contrast between two directions – one is the direction of excessive expression that clings to inordinate knowledge and the second is that of insipid, or shallow, expression that he thinks of in relation to archived or pale or bare knowledge. Somewhere in this contrast what seems to matter is the "touch" of words, but the only way to get to that sense of touch is to see what is at stake for Diamond to which Cavell's essay is a response. Here it might be important to be reminded that, for Cavell, the moments of origin for a thought lie in the provocations among a circle of figures (Cavell 2005: 132); for Cavell, this circle includes Diamond and the ongoing conversations he (Cavell) has with the texts of Wittgenstein. Even if not stated explicitly, somewhere in this conversation is the idea that the touch of words might burn one, in another direction, that one may lose one's touch with words, become a machine, use any word that could efficiently do the work regardless of whether it was a word alive within a form of life, or a frozen word deadened by meaningless repetition? With these ideas in the background, let us see what is at stake in the question of knowledge for Diamond.

A compelling way of posing the issue of violence for Cora Diamond is the issue of what we do to animals in the era of industrial production of animals as food. She takes the violence to animals as one example around what she calls the "difficulty of reality." Diamond pairs this expression with another expression, the "difficulty of philosophy" and in pairing these two expressions she wants to point to a region of ethical, even existential, disquiet that cannot be settled by advancing arguments and counterarguments. In fact, she experiences the urge to offer arguments as itself a form of non-responsiveness, an evasion that is part of her experience of hurt. Cavell is fully attuned to the fact that the wound Diamond speaks of is not the kind of hurt and misunderstanding that arises in the give and take of life, one that we could turn away from, given the right response. Is there a right response?

There is something in certain experiences Diamond feels that is recalcitrant to thought and she can convey such experiences only by means of examples.[10] Stanley Cavell, in his response to Diamond, names this relation between the difficulty of reality and difficulty of philosophy as "inordinate knowledge." It may be worthwhile to consider the examples Diamond gives and then the connections that Cavell makes between the experience of excess, feeling of suffocation, that this kind of knowledge entails that distinguishes it from knowledge that is pale or archived. If "the difficulty of reality" poses certain kinds of problems to philosophy, are these the same kinds of problems it raises for anthropology? Allow me to slow the pace of the thinking here, for the matters raised between Diamond and Cavell are delicate and how one might absorb the problematic in anthropology calls for caution.

Diamond places considerable weight in illustrating what she means by the difficulty of reality by forcefully evoking the cruelties entailed in how we humans treat animals, especially in the context of industrial production of animals as food. Yet she is not speaking as an animal rights advocate, but as one who is mortally wounded, haunted, or maddened by the knowledge of what we do to animals. Diamond takes the example of Mrs. Costello, the protagonist of a novel by J.M. Coetzee, who presented parts of this novel as part of his Tanner lectures on ethics. Mrs. Costello is an elderly woman novelist, a woman "haunted by the horror of what we do to animals." The occasion where the rawness of her nerves is shown is the occasion of a distinguished lecture she has been invited to give in the university where her son teaches. The story unfolds as an unseemly confrontation between the speaker and her audience, especially by the comparison she makes between what we do to animals with the horrors of the Nazi camps. For Diamond, the way to read Coetzee's story is to see it as outside the frame of arguments and counterarguments. Instead, she invites us to think of *how* Coetzee presents a woman whose every word, she claims, is a wound for there is no region of language left untouched by this experience. For many others, Diamond notes, Coetzee is making an argument through a fictional device on how we *should* treat animals. What is the difficulty of reality here?

Our treatment of animals, however, is not the only example Diamond takes. A second example comes from a searing poem by Ted Hughes called "Six Young Men" in which the speaker of the poem is looking at a faded photo from 1914 of these six young men, profoundly and fully alive when the photo was taken, and yet within six months all six were dead in the war. Here is Ted Hughes, saying, "To regard this photograph might well dement." But still, as Diamond says, "It is possible to describe the photo so it does not seem boggling at all" (2008: 44).

So, what is mind boggling in the two examples? At one place in the story of Mrs. Costello, she seems to be deliberately causing offense by making a comparison between the treatment of animals in food factories and the treatment of Jews in Nazi camps. And although the comparison seems obnoxious at first hurried reading, it becomes apparent that she is comparing the claims of ignorance through which many Germans tried to exonerate themselves; and the kinds of justifications many people give of being unaware of the cruel practices carried out in animal farms and their indifference to other humans who are appalled, or wounded by this indifference to them.

Mrs. Costello's lecture (in the novel) includes her statements on this comparison – one of these statements reads: "The crime of the Third Reich, says the voice of accusation, was to treat people like animals ... by treating fellow human beings, created on the image of God, like beasts, they had themselves become beasts." Here lies an important clue for Cavell's statement that how we treat animals is an allegory for how we treat humans. I want to add here, though, that Coetzee is explicit that Mrs. Costello is seeing her fellow human beings as having *become* beastly. In taking offense at her argument, her audience completely misses the point that the slaughterhouse of the animals is seen by her as preparation for human brutality that turns from animals to other humans.

For Diamond then, the joining of the difficulty of reality to the difficulty of philosophy is that philosophy has no means of addressing the wounded speaking animal, except through arguments about rights and personhood, and the most humane ways of killing animals. This is a kind of "as if" engagement: Diamond, using an expression of Cavell's, calls this mode of argumentation a deflection. In Coetzee's novel, Mrs. Costello experiences this terrible rawness of nerves in the kind of questions the audience puts to her; ironically Diamond finds this deflection mirrored in the commentaries on Coetzee's Tanner Lectures, and if one may add in many commentaries on Diamond's essay. (*If* more facts were known, more humane ways of killing would surely evolve [Hacking 2008]; surely the imagination that some can experience animals to be their companions is just part of a putative reality [McDowell 2008].) Against these kinds of arguments, the question for Diamond is: how can we remain indifferent to the fact that some among us experience some animals as their companions, while others can kill and eat them without blinking an eye? This is a question of being unable to imagine an embodied sense of the extinction of another. Our knowledge of our vulnerability to death is wounding *in the light of what we do to animals* both in reality and as an allegory of what we do to each other, as humans.

We might want to be reminded at this point of Diamond's observation that from some perspectives, the examples she offers would not cause any disquiet. But she feels that the entire response to her woundedness offered as erudite arguments is to deflect the issues and inflict hurt of a different order. As an example, I remember discussing with a colleague how I felt unhinged reading some articles in defense of torture after I had heard an almost primitive cry wrenched out from the mother of a torture survivor, and this colleague responding with "different people are entitled to have different views" said sympathetically, yet not connecting to my sense of what was at stake at all. But the difficulty this raises for philosophy, which is that of the impossibility of thinking itself, is of one order – I want to say that the difficulty of what this means to go on within a community, with kin and with neighbors, who have or are suspected to have engaged in killings and rape might be of a different order. I am aware of all the work on forgiveness and reconciliation but with few exceptions most scholars take this work to be that of the individual subject and not of the way the social is brought to bear on these issues or the work of time (see the remarkable work of Osanloo 2020 in this context, though; see also Das 2021).

Most people in the urban slums I work with are not likely to find themselves in lecture halls but they do express themselves publicly. I have written in an earlier book (Das 2007) about the massive violence against members of the Sikh community in Delhi after the assassination of Mrs. Gandhi by her Sikh bodyguards. I worked with the survivors then for more than a year and faced the complete denial on the part of government officials that deaths of Sikh men had taken place at such massive scale in Delhi and elsewhere. I would like to loop back to a description of one of the streets in which killings had happened and the way women sat in silence in these streets as a gesture through which lamenting and cursing were expressed in the excess of the body.

> More powerful than even the words, though, was the way that the women sat in silence outside their houses refusing to bring mourning to an end ... the women were often scared to speak out, but their gestures of mourning that went on and on and on showed the deeply altered meaning of death ... the women defiantly hung on to their filth and their pollution. They would not go into the houses, they would not light the cooking hearths, they would not change their clothes ... the small heaps of ashes (remains of the fires on which bodies were burnt), the abandoned houses, the blood splattered walls created a funeral landscape, the sight of the women with their unwashed bodies and unbraided hair was a potent sign that mourning and protest were part of the same event. (Das 2007: 195)

These were responses carved out of ritual and mythology and embodied the notion of curses on the perpetrators, but also on a world that had allowed such grievous violence to happen. The whole of language was an accusation. I do not know if this kind of difficulty of reality, in which no one could have deciphered what was going on even as the events of murders unfolded over four days, when you could not know in advance which words might betray and which words might save you, your children, your neighbor – is a difficulty of blockages to thought or blockages to living. The response through drawing on mythology and ritual might not be "thought" in the sense that Diamond wants philosophy to respond, but perhaps at the level of the everyday, it was better than "thought." Could mythology and ritual then manage to avoid the disappointment with the forms rational arguments take? Or in other words, could one claim that human expressiveness here finds routes to these difficulties of reality?

It is interesting to me that Diamond does not take up the other registers in Coetzee's novel – for instance the texture of interactions within the domestic scenes when Mrs. Costello realizes that the grandchildren are eating in the playroom because they are going to have chicken soup, and their grandmother does not like meat on the table while their mother does not want to make any concessions to what she calls with obvious irony, her mother-in-law's "delicate sensitivities." In what way would these quotidian interactions change the feeling of abuse that pervades the lecture hall? Mrs. Costello's disappointments are with the philosophers. At one point in the novel she says "Even Immanuel Kant of whom I would have expected better, has a failure of nerve at this point. Even Kant does not pursue, with regard to animals, the implications of his intuition that reason may be not the being of the universe but on the contrary merely the being of the human brain" (Coetzee 2003: 67).

What Diamond makes of this impulse in the novel, however, is something more than the fact that philosophers disappoint her. It is thinking itself which fails in the face of *these* difficulties of reality. But what if we asked, but how do people *live with or endure* such knowledge?

I have seen evidence that makes me put aside the faith in abstract reasoning or in thought experiments to address this particular range of issues pertaining to the moral responsibilities we have to other humans and to animals; I trust simply that, faced with such inordinate knowledge, people did what they could in the circumstances that they found themselves in. I recall the way in which the pressure generated by policemen to provide false witness against the accused arrested under terror laws was resisted (not always successfully) as families would send homemade food, a hand-knitted scarf, a letter, a picture drawn by a child, across the prison walls made up of brick and mortar, and of the thick lattice of police procedures, knowing full well that the prisoner will be mocked for these, that these gifts would be seized on one pretext or another, but *willing* the prisoner to know that he is loved. This is the register of words, gestures, and their physiognomy that I have tried to give expression to in this work. As an anthropologist and in fidelity to those in these urban slums I have come to know, I would say that the power of such gestures and of words as gestures is that they do not engage in the kinds of arguments Mrs. Costello was confronted with during the course of her lecture. After all, they have to live in neighborhoods in which your next-door neighbor might be a police informer; or, it may be a kinsman who gave false evidence against your husband or son in a terror trial either out of fear or because of greed; or, a child might say something that would identify a secret you were trying to hide from the police and so words have to be guarded, or perhaps covered up with euphemisms. But in the very ways in which excess of expression and concealment of it are made part of these lives, they testify to the different ways in which people learn to live with inordinate knowledge.

The Next Chapters

The following chapters are not organized around each of these issues separately – rather the questions I opened the book with run through the book like streams that run into each other throughout. I give here, a brief account of what to expect in the following chapters.

Chapter 2, "The Catastrophic Event: Enduring Inordinate Knowledge," analyzes the manner in which catastrophic events, namely the Bombay successive blasts in March 1993 and the Bombay train bomb blasts of 2006, unfold within the law, asking what kinds of police practices do these events bring to light? Such practices, I argue, fracture not only individual lives but also the life of the community. At the level of the law, I analyze the vast number of documents produced in the process of terror trials of the 1993 bomb blasts in the TADA[11] courts and show that a focus away from the final judgment to the more minor documents such as police affidavits, bail petitions, petitions opposing extension of police custody, as well as confessions elicited from the accused, reveal the fictions of the law. A close reading of these documents yields important insights into the judicial processes through which torture can take place right under the eyes of the judges and within the legal processes itself. Although very few legal scholars would now accept Bentham's characterization of common law fictions as "wicked falsehoods," not every type of conceptual construction can be brought under the label of a legal fiction (see Del Mar and Twining 2015). The chapter shows in some detail how specific devices of fiction, such as plot, character, and chronotope, are used to create a story of conspiracy which even if it is not upheld for all the accused over time, nevertheless produces enough opportunities for torture, intimidation, harassment of the accused and their respective kin and friends, while also blurring the distinction between a suspect and a witness.

The second moment of the argument in the chapter is an exposition of a stunning book written by Abdul Wahid Shaikh who was one of the accused in the bomb blasts of July 11, 2006 (popularly known as 7/11), in which there was a simultaneous explosion of seven bombs planted in the train plying between Churchgate and Virar stations of Western railways in Mumbai. I argue that this book demonstrates the importance of vernacular writings that I honor for informing social theory. Written as a pedagogy of the oppressed, and drawing from experiences of Muslim subjects brought into the grip of law and subjected to torture, Abdul Wahid Shaikh's book is a manual for how to behave under torture, how to withdraw your words when needed, and when to shout them out, even if they are going unheard. *Begunah Qaidi* (*The innocent prisoner*) does not provide a learned genealogy of techniques of torture of the kind that Rejali (2007) provides in his meticulously researched book on torture and democracy, but it has an eye for detail that shows the cunning of the social character of torture as technique within the judicial process. To take a simple example, many English-speaking people when in a police station might easily miss the *patta*, the leather belt hanging in police stations that are used normally in mechanical grinders. These are used to beat up suspects and there is a black humor in the inscriptions on these belts, recalling titles of popular Bollywood films. But the existence and use of such *pattas* was common knowledge among many who lived in the slums. Some of these people might have actually experienced a beating at the hands of an inebriated policeman before being let off with the offering of a bribe. Others might have just heard rumors about such objects. Still others knew how these kinds of punishments might morph into second- or third-degree torture if they became implicated in an infamous case that went beyond local petty crimes. Shaikh's book describes such events with a clinical detachment and provides a more convincing refutation of the learned discourses on justifications for torture offered by law professors of elite universities, or arguments on the "civilized" or "rational" violence of the state, than any sophisticated thought experiment I could have constructed to counter the ticking-bomb scenario of these discussions or the hand-wringing around good people having to do bad things and dirty their hands.

Chapter 3, "The Dispersed Body of the Police and Fictions of the Law," takes the textures of everyday relations in the slums and tracks how the policing functions get dispersed over a range of actors. Similar to Foucault's insight that the body of the psychiatrist is present in the tokens of his power that are displayed everywhere in the asylum, or in the actions of servants whose work is conceptualized as an extension of the medical gaze, I found that the presence of the police was widely dispersed in different social actors. While some aspects of policing might be understood by following formal police patrols or by seeing what transpires in police stations in, say, the recording of FIRs, for other aspects to come to light a methodological push would be needed to expand the boundaries of the field site by either following the same cases over a period of time, or by keeping track of the different places one might find policemen or policewomen within the communities or neighborhoods they are entrusted to police. For instance, even when the local constabulary was supposed to make "rounds" of the neighborhood in Delhi, they rarely went into the narrower meandering streets (*galis*), confining themselves to visiting the houses of the known political leaders or of middlemen and of women who were already in an awkward relation to normative kinship and who acted as intermediaries. One purpose of this chapter is to show how this dispersed body of the police secretes certain realities that function in one way at the level of low-income neighborhoods, and quite another way when a case is propelled into more formal spaces such as in courts of law. At the level of neighborhoods and slums that are defined as crime-prone, the police use informers, the local dons, and the readily available mafia-like figures as their eyes and ears. These routes through which power flows in the everyday life of the community creates widespread distrust of neighbors or even kin, but the lines of skepticism regarding the trustworthiness of relations in the neighborhood are not given once and for all and are continually realigned in view of new experiences. I describe a case of abduction and rape of a child that does manage to reach the courts by tracking the life of minor documents that are generated from within the community and leave their traces on the documents that are finally produced in court. Taking the theme of legal fictions further, this chapter shows that legal fictions are not simply devices in the hands of judges and lawyers but have different lives in a network of interconnected spaces and times. I find it particularly interesting that these small tools of knowledge (e.g., police memos, police diaries, spot reports) reveal how one part of the functioning of the law can remain opaque to other parts of the juridical process.

Chapter 4, "Detecting the Human: Under Which Skies Do We Theorize?," asks how do we think of the limits of the human not as a metaphysical issue, but one as it arises within a weave of life? The inhuman as a limit of the human, I argue, lies not in monstrosities produced by nature or in evil inherent in men and women, but in the machines that provide the affordances for the inhuman to become one eventuality of the human.

In his profound reflections on the extreme violence of genocide, Rechtman (2020, 2021) says with devastating simplicity, monstrosity lies not in the person but in the incommensurability that the "evil" of totalitarianism, its stupendous violence, is enabled and served by the hands of completely mediocre men, and I would want to add, not under conditions of totalitarianism alone.

How, then, are we to think of the imperatives to give expression to this experience of inhumanity I found in the slums? The question, as Cavell (1979) has phrased it, is not how society provides correction to *its* soul as a picture of one's being within a form of life, of the knitting of the interior and the exterior; it is, rather, how does the soul find ways of correcting *its* society? It is in response to this question that I look at ethnographic moments, the story written by a child, a mother's primitive cry as expressing how she experienced her son's torture, four friends watering the fragile plant of friendship across the Hindu-Muslim divide in a politically fraught environment, as examples of the ways of a soul finding *its* society. These are also moments that are woven into the becoming of an anthropologist, or into the kind of anthropologist I have become.

The Conclusion should help the voices that have emerged in this text through the intimacy between this writer and the lives and texts she has lived with, to circle back to this very moment in the Introduction as one must return repeatedly to the experience of being in the middle of things, and being within a circle of figures of thought.

2
The Catastrophic Event: Enduring Inordinate Knowledge

Let me start with a very quotidian, everyday experience, that of arriving in any of these neighborhoods described in the Introduction. Initially people show great curiosity about what you are doing there and often try to offer guesses "Are you from an NGO?," "Is there any government scheme you have come to publicize?," "Are you registering names for plot allotments?," "What's happening?," and as you are trailed by curious young men, women, and children or greeted by women sitting on their doorsteps, you feel you are not unwelcome. People in these areas have become used to NGOs, journalists, market researchers coming in and out and they can be very articulate in giving answers to their questions. Yet even after you have got to know them, any conversation might touch on more difficult terrain, such as a case of a contested arrest, or the discovery of a dead body, or a story that has broken in a newspaper about a suicide, and the faces go blank as the standard response is offered – *humen nahin pata, hum to ji apne kaam se matlab rakhte hain*, "we don't know we are just concerned with our own work," implying that they keep themselves to themselves despite the density of houses and the cheek by jowl existence the residents lead. Ultimately it is just by hanging around, or helping out when small and big problems arise, that trust might be slowly won, though as is proper, one must try to let the knowledge of what is going on come to one rather than force any confidences.

Building on these casual observations, I want to think of how catastrophic events produce forms of knowledge that might circulate in the slums but are usually handled with euphemisms, evasions, and even silence. Such forms of knowing are, on the one hand, difficult to give expression to, and on the other hand, they are excessive in their implications for revealing aspects of life that are often veiled or shrouded in layers of obfuscations and euphemisms. Stanley Cavell (2008, 2010), as we saw, called this register of knowing, inordinate knowledge, dangerous not because it is hidden but because we don't dare to acknowledge it. I would like to propose that how we absorb such knowledge within the discipline of anthropology, overcoming the urge to master it and yet allowing our work to be marked by such registers of knowing, might be one way that anthropology might render its understanding of "slum acts" and find its bearings as it navigates what Cora Diamond memorably called the "difficulty of reality" and the "difficulty of philosophy" as we discussed in the Introduction (Cavell 2007a; Diamond 2003, 2008).

I suggested in the last chapter that the "difficulty of philosophy" that unsettles Diamond might become anchored to a different emotional valence in the lives of communities portrayed here, since the question shifts from the difficulty of philosophy to the difficulty of living or carrying inordinate knowledge when you know life has to be lived in the environment of suspicion, fear, and pervasive skepticism about the truth of one's relations. Let us recall that in his characterization of inordinate knowledge, Stanley Cavell (2010) described it as "excessive in its expression" and contrasted it with knowledge that is "mere or bare or pale or intellectualized, uninsistent, inattentive, distracted, filed, archived" (Cavell 2010: 84). Yet, I hope to show in the discussion that follows that the boundaries between what knowledge is pale or bare and what it is that comes to carry the possibilities of excessive expression does not lie in any absolute characteristic of forms of knowledge. Rather, it is the way in which knowledge of one's relationships enters the realms of the social, becomes weighty with consequences for those who are in possession of knowledge or for those who have to endure what they cannot ignore, that it moves from being pale and bare to dark and filled with plenitude. Thus, a legal document might appear as pale and archived knowledge in a dusty official archive, yet when we take such documents back and place them within the forms of life in which they once existed, we can decipher the excess that must have given them the character of dangerous documents carrying in themselves the power over life and death. Taking forward Sandra Laugier's (2020) brilliant formulation that ordinary language is best seen as a site of human expressivity, a mixture of foreignness and familiarity, I might say here that the language that comes into being in relation to something catastrophic bringing in its wake the foreignness of, say, institutions of the state, new aspects of life which one might have only vaguely sensed, but which lurked in one's milieu, cannot be precisely defined. The circulation of such knowledge, not among anonymous publics marked by stranger sociality, but within the thick of one's relationships, might reveal an awakening to possibilities of peril one might have only dimly perceived earlier, and the burden on inhabitants of these milieus to assimilate such knowledge within the folds of everyday life.

The catastrophic events I take up in this chapter are the Bombay (now Mumbai) bomb blasts punctuated over several years (1993, 2003, 2006, 2008, 2011). For many scholars, the bomb blasts were one link in a chain of preceding events that all indexed the growth of Hindu nationalism and riots and pogroms against Muslim minorities (Ghassem-Fachandi 2012); many of these scholars also argue that a new kind of politics was initiated in which the bomb blasts would increasingly be placed within a global story of Islamophobia, urban disorder, and terrorist violence (Rao 2007).

I don't disagree with these formulations but I am suggesting an opposite move. I am aware that the terror trials which followed the bomb blasts produced hundreds of stories of the nexus between the film industry and the underworld in Bombay, corrupt politicians and police, and the growing menace of terrorism. Still, certain stories remained understated. These were the stories of the hundreds of minor characters who came within the net of the law as they faced charges of being accomplices in the terror attacks. Most of these minor actors were from the chawls, and the low-income Muslim localities (although some of the accused were Hindus or Muslims from elite families), who might have been involved in a plethora of small acts of cheating, smuggling, or money laundering, but mostly they were leading ordinary lives marked by what I have called a certain normativity honed out of the pathology of these places, for it is near impossible to live ordinary lives here without having broken some law or other (see Das 2015, 2020). If the city of Bombay seems like the protagonist of this story of bomb blasts, there were other places to which networks of human and nonhuman agents were traced and which came to impact on the lives of these slum dwellers by further fraying their networks of relations and depositing in their lives lethal memories, impossible conflicts, which they survived but which imbued everyday life with betrayals and disappointments, that might have corroded already fragile relations among neighbors, kin, and others in whose proximity life had to be resumed.

The Event

Let us consider the first of these events. The Bombay bomb blasts were successive blasts which started on March 12, 1993, on the last Friday of Ramadan in Bombay (later renamed Mumbai) in the basement of the Bombay Stock Exchange and then moved in a series of coordinated explosions to such iconic buildings as the Air India Building, Sea Rock hotel, and Plaza Cinema. The date, March 12, was later named "Black Friday" and became the subject of many literary and cinematic productions. The powerful explosions left 257 people dead and 1,400 injured. The main culprits in this case were said to be the underworld dons, Dawood Ibrahim, and Tiger Memon. Both accused, however, escaped. Tiger Memon's younger brother Yakub Memon was apprehended and after a trial under the special TADA court, he was found guilty and executed by hanging on July 30, 2015. Other siblings were tried and either acquitted for lack of evidence or given life terms in prison, but the state was not able to apprehend the main accused Tiger Memon and Ibrahim Dawood though cases for their extradition continue in various courts in different countries. The story of the 1993 bomb blasts has received much attention in popular media and in scholarly discussions but the focus has been on the main accused. Yet there were (depending on how we count them) 84 to 100 other persons, minor characters to be sure, who were named in the charge sheets for a variety of roles they are said to have played in the conspiracy to erode "the sovereignty and integrity" of India. Many of the accused were later released with warnings or acquitted for lack of evidence, but their stories have not received much attention. I am interested in making a case for looking at several minor documents to trace how police procedures transformed these minor characters in the story as if they were essential cogs in the machinery of terrorism, part of a major conspiracy to challenge the sovereignty and territorial integrity of India. What can we learn by paying attention to these characters about (a) the deep embrace of law and force (legal and illegal) within the story of sovereignty, and (b) the consequences of their legal transformation into big-time terrorists through police and court procedures upon their relations and on the delicate balance of sustaining life among kin and among their neighboring communities versus protecting themselves and their immediate family?

Two Ways of Deciphering a Terror Trial

Given the opacity of an event such as a series of bomb blasts in a city, it is not surprising that such an event opens up several routes through which one might interpret its meaning and significance. Without necessarily being able to pronounce on the merits of one or other view, I think that each route of interpretation homes in on a sensibility which is at least in part a result of one's location and one's experiences – each mode of interpretation finds room for some experiences while it shuts others off. As will become evident, I am rather more inclined to give a privileged place to the experiences I find encoded in the minor documents I mentioned and concentrate on the minor actors who appeared in the documents and, in most cases, disappeared from the final judgments.

The first mode of interpretation which looks at the big story is captured in an elegant paper entitled "How to read a bomb" by Vyjayanthi Rao (2007), in which she argues that the protagonist of this story is none other than the city of Bombay itself. The bomb blasts are placed in a series marked by a place and a time – a spatio-temporal configuration perhaps best described in terms of Bakhtin's (1982) concept of a chronotope as a literary device through which the plot moves so that different layers of an event within a novel are revealed (see also Lawson 2011). Bakhtin was interested in asking what are the conditions in a novel that allow two characters to meet and, in a reverse move, what happens when they miss each other? Though Rao does not evoke Bakhtin, her analysis seems to be analogous to Bakhtin's in that we could ask, what makes the bomb meet the city? Let us zoom in at certain moments within the prose of Rao's elegant essay:

> The apparent lack of an identifiable perpetrator, given that unmanned mobile vehicles had served as the agents of the detonations, the lack of discrimination in choosing victims, created a very estranged sense of "cityness" in the aftermath of the blasts. (pp. 570–1)

Further on:

> The city appeared without individuality or particularity – without boundaries, without the recognition of an inside or an outside, of an enemy, or another, but as a pure instance of victimhood. It was, as well, a specifically global moment, for the city as it joined what were the areas similarly targeted by acts of terrorist violence. (p. 571)

One has to applaud Rao for not immediately falling into the trap of reading into the event the motives of the terrorists, which Talal Asad (2007) has critiqued in his astute and compelling arguments as revealing more about the compulsions of the commentators on suicide bombers rather than about the persons committing such acts. Instead, Rao opts for capturing what middle-class residents might have felt as currents of feeling without identifiable agents or subjects swept the city. When agents appear in Rao's account as a result of the investigations, they are quickly assimilated into the familiar tropes of gangsters and the underworld. For instance, she writes: "An early breakthrough in the investigation revealed that one of the vehicles used for the bombing – one that had failed to detonate – was registered in the name of a relative of Mustaq Memon, a Mumbai gangster popularly known as Tiger Memon. The clue led to further revelations of the extent to which the famed Bombay underworld, a territorializing and extrajudicial force to reckon with in its own right – had been involved in the bombings (Rao 2007: 574–5). Rao reveals, almost as an aside, that in early days following the bomb blasts 200 people were initially arrested of whom 100 were eventually charged for active complicity in various acts such as detonating the bombs, taking part in planning meetings in several cities such as Dubai and Karachi, landing of guns, and explosives in Mumbai through known smuggler routes, *hawala* transactions for financing, and so on. It is these lattices of criminal acts that were supposed to have made the bomb blasts possible and hence were brought under the category of terrorist acts rather than individual crimes at different levels of severity.

This is the point at which I think we could stop and ask some questions. For instance, how does the theoretical move to think of the city as the "pure victim" serve to move the author's gaze to a place where any discussion of the techniques used by the police to make "facts" appear are completely taken on trust? As in the public sphere, so in this text, "The clues led to further revelations" gives us a sense of security that police investigations are trustworthy. But, which clues?

Offered by whom? Produced how and where? The "global moment" in which she places the city as "pure victim" elides the real presence of the chawls and the low-income localities from where most of the accused came. Had some attention been paid to tracking these real people, it might have helped Rao to see through the language that appears in police documents as well as in many media accounts. Instead, Rao's language here comes so close to the language that the police were to deploy in the various affidavits before courts asking for extension of the period of police custody for the accused, or creating a story of Muslim hurt and revenge in which every plot point carefully charts out the chronotope through which the very images of global terror, revenge, unknown perpetrators, the city as victim, is produced. There are uncanny resonances between police language and scholarly prose. Let us then turn to a second way of reading how to think of bomb explosions and terrorist assemblages in the city that seems both more modest and more grounded.

The legal scholar Mayur Suresh (2016, 2019) goes to the heart of the matter of the very question I have posed here, namely, how is legal truth produced? On the basis of a case study of a terrorism trial in Delhi in 2008, Suresh makes a compelling argument that TADA courts may have been instituted under the legal provisions for exceptional cases, but the judicial logic produced during the adjudication process is very similar to what happens in the case of ordinary crimes. In both cases, judicial truth is both produced and contested in the course of the trial by a production of files and by processes of certification which include very humble acts such as verifications of signatures, producing memos to document an act deemed essential, and so on. Examples of such documents include memos certified by an eyewitness of, say, a moment at which the accused led the police to the spot from which a weapon was recovered, or the recording of confessions through due procedure and the production of such documents duly inscribed in the police diary which documents the actual processes of investigation. In Suresh's felicitous phrasing, "bureaucratic documentary practices produce objects and people – files also produce time and narrative" (2019: 177, see also Vismann 2008). Suresh adds the important qualification that the narrative is not produced at any particular moment, say at the time that the judgment is delivered in a final synthesis; rather, "narratives in a case are a sum of smaller narratives dispersed through the documentary record" (2019: 178).

In the case study that Suresh provides us, he shows how the defense counsel for an accused in the bomb blast case in Delhi in 2008, for instance, is able to argue on the basis of the contradictions in the narrative about the investigation itself that the police had made up a story of a spot map, claiming it to be a record of what was witnessed at the site but the contradictions of time and space show that it must have been recorded later in the police station. Since the police could produce no independent witnesses in this case, the history of the investigation provided the clue to the conclusion that the spot report was indeed prepared later, not at the scene, but at the police station. Suresh's demonstration that the files mediate different versions of reality is well argued but I think one can go further and show how important it is for the police to build a plausible story and that elements of fiction are crucial for deciphering these humble texts for claims and counterclaims about "facts" produced during the course of the trial.

The Bombay Bomb Blasts

Let us return to the 1993 Bombay bomb blasts and see what the perusal of the minor documents that were generated in the course of the court trials can tell us about these blasts that takes not the city as the protagonist of the story but some of the minor characters. There is a puzzle here as to why the police apparatus is deployed to create the story of a major conspiracy when the police officers are well aware that most of the people arrested on suspicion will be acquitted in the end for lack of evidence, although it may take a decade or even two decades to arrive at that point. Let us keep this question at the back of our mind because it will lead us into the whole issue of the kind of knowledge secreted through such procedures that seeps into the everyday life of communities and acquires the character of inordinate knowledge with which I started this chapter.

India has a vast legal apparatus, geared towards the governance of exceptions, that works as a parallel system to deal with conditions of "disorder" either in areas defined as "disturbed" areas within the country, or to contain specific types of dangers emanating from groups defined as "insurgents," "terrorists," "militants," and are seen to constitute specific risks to "public safety" (Raman 2017). The assumption behind this parallel legal apparatus is that a distinction between ordinary crime and extraordinary violations necessitates a legal apparatus such as special courts, and extraordinary legislative provisions to protect the sovereignty and territorial integrity of India. From the Preventive Detention Act, 1950, through TADA (The Terrorist and Disruptive Activities (Prevention) Act, 1985 and 1987) to POTA (Prevention of Terrorism Act, 2001), there is a patchwork of federal laws that have jurisdiction over what are defined as crimes against the sovereignty of the country. In addition, there are state-level laws in different parts of the country such as the MCOCA (Maharashtra Control of Organized Crime Act, 1999) in Maharashtra, which continue to function as extraordinary legal provisions with separate jurisdiction even after repeal of federal laws. The problems of jurisdiction of these courts and their relation to fundamental rights, such as the right to life, have come up for discussion in a number of impressive scholarly writings (see, for instance, Ahmad 2017; Baxi 2005; Lokaneeta 2011; Singh 2006, 2007). One of the important points made in this literature is that, despite the attempt to separate the extraordinary laws from the operation of ordinary laws, in fact there is a spillage between the two. For instance, courts have been at pains to draw strict boundaries between the two types of jurisdiction, yet evidence obtained in one type of case (e.g., a confession or a recovery of a weapon) seems to slip into evidence elicited in another case. Important though the analysis of legal judgments in these cases is, I want to move away from the final judgment to the interim issues that come up in various petitions before the courts on such issues as bail applications, or petitions to ask for termination of orders for daily reporting at the police station when someone is on bail.

I hope to show the importance of these petitions as most cases linger in courts for years and I argue that the passing of time here is not a simple duration leading to the final judgment. Rather, there is a different kind of work with time that is being performed. As Bourdieu (1990: 106–7) said of gift-exchange, and Suresh (2019) of court trials, time has to be seen as active and agential. For instance, in the case of the 1993 Bombay bomb blasts, the bomb explosions took place on March 12, 1993, but the final judgment of the courts was delivered only on March 21, 2013. There are special provisions in the terror-related legislative acts that give a lot of leeway to the police in the investigative process which makes it imperative to see how one might read the variety of legal documents (and not only the final judgments) to decipher the impact that these police procedures have on the communities from which the accused come.

I should note here that most cases tried under the terror-related laws start with a large number of people who are arrested and put under police or judicial custody. Even when, in the end, many of these persons under suspicion are released, they have been subjected to physical abuse, intimidation, torture, and attempts by the police to use their relatives and friends as witnesses against them. One of the consequences of such tactics is often that relations between kin and between neighbors are eroded. Hence the unusual step I take to concentrate on the minor characters and smaller stories grafted onto the main story, rather than looking at the big men such as the underworld bosses who were found in the final judgments to be the main culprits. However, one might want to keep one important fact in mind: namely, that during the time that TADA was operative (1985–95), 77,500 persons were arrested of whom 25% were released without any formal charges by the police, and of the 35% that were brought to court, 95% were acquitted for lack of supporting evidence. Less than 2% of those arrested were convicted. Furthermore, the literature is littered with examples of the flimsy evidence that was used to seek convictions and was admitted under TADA courts.

Let us recall here that after 20 years of judicial proceedings on the 1993 Bomb blast case, the supreme court gave its judgment on March 21, 2013, upholding the death sentence against suspected ringleader Yakub Memon, while commuting the previous death sentences against ten other defendants to life in prison. Instead of looking at the final judgments, I propose to look at what Suresh (2019) called the humble documents to ask what exactly transpired in this period. While I will take up the cases of two minor characters, Ahsan Mohammad Qureshi and Shaikh Salim Mustafa Shaikh who were ultimately acquitted, let me first give a sense of two types of documents that were produced by the police in the course of the trials: one is the supposed confessional statement, and the second is the affidavit by a police officer, either contesting a bail application or asking for extension of the period of police custody or judicial custody for the accused.[1] As I hope to show, both types of document seem to be written within a particular plot structure in which different kinds of fictions – counterfactuals, chronotope, logical (as opposed to real) possibilities – are marshalled to create a story that is geared toward buying time rather than necessarily getting a conviction. In that sense, Suresh's depiction is spot on that the courts produce not only persons and objects but also time and narrative.

The Confession

On the basis of a close reading of the 60 confessional statements that I was able to find in cases registered with TADA courts in connection with the 1993 bomb blasts, it seems to me that the confessional statements secured two objectives. First, there is a common plot which consists of certain key components, such as a plotting of times and spaces, which would build a plausible story that a person, say living in a low-income locality and working in the capacity of an office-boy, or working as a cleaner in a soft-drink company on a salary of Rs. 1500 per month (approx. $30 at 1993 rates), and who has studied up to seventh or eighth grade, would have come into contact with the main accused who were well-known Dons with properties in affluent areas in Mumbai, Dubai, and other cities. How to conjure a plausible story of conspiracy through which different kinds of spaces (streets with million-dollar sprawling bungalows and the narrow, winding streets in the chawls) can come together in the same narrative as sites of collaboration rather than mutual exclusion? The elaboration of this theme creates a geography on which low-income workers steeped in poverty are lured into becoming part of the terrorist machine and are sent to Pakistan for training, or Dubai for being whetted by the leaders to see if they are suitable for the roles being assigned to them. In some cases, the confessions give the impression of willing compliance with roles assigned; in others, the person speaks of threats and compulsions and, as we will see later, these variations relate to the different techniques through which confessions were obtained.

The second aspect of the confessions is a common story of a chain of events starting with the destruction of the Babri mosque[2] and subsequent riots in Mumbai in which Muslim lives and property were damaged, and a consequent incitement to revenge to which poor Muslims became particularly susceptible, or so the storyline is crafted. For example, in one of the confessional statements, AG, who is a hawker, is asked:

> All those weapons. (Chemicals, ammuniation [*sic*] was brought by Tiger and his companions . . . then all those kept before you, fitted them before you . . . By which intention did you do all this? What do you understand/know about this?

He replies:

> All those weapons, Chemicals, ammuniation [*sic*] were brought for taking the revenge of the riots, which took place in the month of December 1992, and January, 1993

in which Muslims were suffered [*sic*] damage of property
and were burnt and killed.

Other components of the story relate to what I can
only assume to be a picture of Muslim subjects as "religious," for all such confessions to which I had access
included one segment in which new recruits are made
to take an oath keeping their hands on the holy Quran
and saying in unison that they will not divulge anything
that transpires to any outsider and that they would in
all fidelity (*imaan*) wage jihaad on the *kafirs*. I found
only two confessional statements in which the earlier
confession is rescinded on the grounds that the accused
had been beaten or tortured and compelled to sign false
confessions. However, we will see later through the
revelations in a courageous memoir pertaining to the
July 11, 2006, Mumbai train blast case that torture was
regularly used in the prisons to extract confessions in
most terror trials. One may note here that the admissibility of a confession made to a police officer higher than
the Superintendent of Police was a provision of special
laws to deal with terrorism under TADA and later
POTA, since in the ordinary course of criminal trials
confessions made before a police officer are not admissible as evidence. Section 25 of the Indian Evidence Act
makes any confession made in the presence of a police
officer inadmissible as evidence of crime, while section
26 enjoins that a confession made by a person while
in police custody is admissible if the confession was
made in the presence of a magistrate. Thus, in treating
"clues" gathered through police investigations with suspicion, we might begin to parse the victims of the bomb
explosions as consisting not only of those who died as
a result of the explosions but also as those whose lives
were severely disrupted by the police procedures and
the imperative to create a story of police vigilance and a

whole country under threat from terrorist violence. I do not mean to say that the threat of terrorism both from the transnational networks and from the police is not real, but in these cases the crimes did not amount to putting the sovereignty and integrity of the country at risk. The story of a widespread conspiracy enabled the police to bring many innocent Muslims under the purview of terrorist trials, sometimes by conflating the category of minor crimes with terrorist crimes, and at other times conflating the witness with the accused.[3]

The Bail Petition

Out of the 84 accused of being part of a grand conspiracy of attacking the sovereignty and integrity of the country as presented in court, let me select two minor actors, Ahsan Mohammad Qureshi, who owned a small business, and a worker in his shop, Shaikh Salim Mustafa Shaikh. Appearing as accused number 46 and accused no. 47, the charges against them were similar, namely that they had used a Maruti vehicle for disposal of arms and ammunition in Mahim Creek. It was alleged in Ahsan's case that one pistol and 16 live rounds were found in his possession. Salim was, however, made out to be an accomplice merely on the grounds that he was a close friend of Ahsan and one other accused. Unlike a large number of cases in which the accused were charged with having travelled to Dubai or Pakistan to receive training, or to move money or weapons, these two were charged only with having aided in disposing of arms and ammunition.

I don't intend to trace here the trajectory of the whole case that was tried in the TADA court, but to take us through two specific moments – first, when a bail application was filed on behalf of the petitioners against the State of Maharashtra, with the senior police inspector at the Worli Police Station as the main respondent. The application was moved on November 24, 1993. This was followed by another application for removing the case from the jurisdiction of TADA on December 13 and 14. What interests me in these bail petitions is the structure of reasoning for denial of bail and the arguments on jurisdiction offered by the respondent – the chief investigating officer. Let us first see the main claim made by the petitioner which goes as follows:

> While the petitioner submits and states that on March 12, 1993, there were a series of bomb blasts in Bombay, he avers that he had no connection directly or indirectly, with the same. Furthermore, no case has been made out against him by the state in their affidavits. The petitioner has many close friends and associates not only from his community but from the majority community . . . no weapons were recovered from his person, office, or home by the police, as also averred by the police officer . . . the petitioner was arrested on April 5, 1993 and was in police custody, in wrongful confinement, up to May 24, 1993, i.e., for 49 days. As the police were not able to make out any case against him, he was remanded in judicial custody on May 24, 1993, itself. The learned judge of the designated court had incarcerated him into judicial custody as the investigations by the police are over, as far as he is concerned.

The petition goes on to make the case that the only evidence the police claimed to have against the accused was that he had been in possession of an unlicensed foreign marked pistol which another accused, Feroze, had purportedly either given or sold him. "In any case," says the submission, "this would not come under the scope of TADA act but would have to be viewed under the 'arms act'."

Next, let us consider the affidavits filed by the investigating officer. I don't reproduce the affidavits in their entirety but zoom into the following kinds of statements.

- "It is obvious that the petition is filed with oblique motive which is obviously to stall the investigation which is in full force."
- "It is true that no weapon, ammunition, were recovered by the police. However, police recovered one foreign marked pistol and 16 cartridges explosives. It is true that the weapon was not used but the accused had thrown the said foreign marked pistol and 16 cartridges in Mahim creek from where these weapons were recovered."
- "The present petitioner has links with the underworld and he attempted to destroy the evidence that linked him to the conspiracy."
- "It is true that the petitioner was remanded in judicial custody on May 24, 1993 but it cannot be inferred that the investigation is completed. It is reiterated that though the police have arrested 84 persons, they have yet to trace a number of culprits. Interrogation of those arrested led the investigative machinery to trace the real culprits and arrest them."
- "The possibility cannot be ruled out that if they are *minutely interrogated*, it will be possible to get information regarding the participation of other wanted accused persons. Even chances are within sight to seize more material."

I doubt that we need any subtle analysis of these statements to decipher that (i) there is no attempt to distinguish far-fetched possibilities from real possibilities; (ii) the phrase "minutely interrogated" truly refers to subjecting the accused who are under police custody and without the right to have lawyers present during these "minute" interrogations, to physical beatings, and first, if not second degree torture; and (iii) the purpose is to extract names of people who can be arrested on the grounds that their names came up on the interrogation of those already arrested. These interpretations are not far-fetched. The reason that, when produced by the police before the judges to seek extension of the period of police custody and asked if the prisoner has any complaints, the prisoner inevitably replies in the negative, is that they have been warned that any complaint before the judge would lead to more beatings and torture, arrest of the person's relatives or close friends, and much worse besides.

In his interim order on the bail application, the judge pointed out that there were no grounds for extension of police custody. As the judge ruled, even if the accused had a criminal background and belonged to underground groups like SIMI,[4] and had acquired a weapon in a clandestine way, their motive in acquiring a weapon was to engage in gang warfare in order to emerge as unrivalled bullies – it was not to strike terror in the minds of people and to disrupt the sovereignty and territorial integrity of the country. However, such is the pressure on judges to show their patriotism, that the judge added, "I do not think that so far as these two are concerned, there is anything left to be investigated and probably they had been arrested and charged for offenses under TADA by way of abundant precaution." Months after Qureshi and Shaikh had been on bail, their respective lawyers filed another petition to discontinue the requirement for their having to report to the police station every day, and to remove the case from the jurisdiction of the TADA court.

I want to pause for a moment here before I go to the next section to bring out the different registers in which the main advocate, Mr. B. speaks in these petitions – with dramatic accusations against politicians and police that, however, remain indefinite – and request for relief from various quotidian hardships to which his client is being subjected. Here is a quotation from one of the petitions he files:

Sadly enough, not only have there been allegations, which are often not unfounded, of an alleged nexus existing between the enforcers of the law, some prominent bureaucrats and some professional politicians with the law breakers and underworld, but also of reckless use of draconian TADA regulations predictably resulting in an abuse of power and law by over-enthusiastic and/or corrupt enforcers of law.

And then the register completely shifts into the quotidian:

Their having to report to the DCB (CID) every day is taking a heavy toll on their business. Since Applicant No. 1 has a large number of family members and dependents to support, it has become very difficult for him to spend much time in his business, as everyday he has to make a long haul to the DCB – hours away from his workplace.

What this petition is not able to mention is that there is never a guarantee that when you present yourself at the DCB, you will not be beaten up, disappeared, or killed in an encounter with the false charge of having threatened a police officer. It was not possible for me to trace any of the accused who were acquitted in the 1993 trials,[5] but Abdul Wahid Shaikh, who was arrested in the 7/11 case of train bomb blasts in 2006 and spent nine years in prison (being the only one of the 12 accused to be finally acquitted), uses delicate irony to tell this aspect of the story. He told me of a phone call he recently received from the same police officer who had been in charge of his investigation. Inviting him to come to the police station for a cup of tea, the police officer said, "Why are you persisting with complaints to human rights tribunals against us? After all what is over is over. Why don't we have a friendly chat over a cup of tea – after all, we all have to live together (*rehna to ek saath hi hai na?*)." Shaikh had replied, "Sir, the last time I was invited to a cup of tea, I spent nine years in jail and was beaten up and tortured. If you want me to come to the police station you will have to send me a formal summons – I am not coming for any tea." Let us then go on to see how Wahid Shaikh theorized his own experiences in the nine long years that he spent as an accused in a terror case. It might be helpful to keep in mind the case I made in the Introduction for treating texts produced at the local level and vernacular languages as an essential component of subjugated knowledge. These are part of my education in the social sciences, not simply data for our own theorization.

Begunah Qaidi: The Innocent Prisoner

Abdul Wahid Shaikh, the author of the piercing analysis of terror trials in his book, *Begunah Qaidi (The Innocent Prisoner*, 2017) was one of the accused in the bomb blasts on July 11, 2006, in which there was a simultaneous explosion of seven bombs planted on the train plying between Churchgate and Virar stations of Western Railways, all between 6.23 and 6.28 in the evening when commuters were returning home. There were 188 deaths and 817 people were injured. Charges were first filed in different lower courts and were finally transferred to the special MCOCA court. Thirteen Muslim men were arrested and charged, while a further 15 could not be apprehended and were reported to be in Pakistan or Nepal. Two of the accused who had escaped to Pakistan were reported dead. The only person acquitted of the charges was Abdul Wahid Shaikh. It is to his book that I turn now to show the characteristics of the powerful critique he provides.[6]

Wahid Shaikh was acquitted of all charges in September 2015 after he had spent nearly a decade in prison. He wrote *Begunah Qaidi* while in prison but, unlike the texts of famous political prisoners in India, the author wrote it while being subjected to torture, intimidation and threats to his family, and repeated attempts by the police to break his spirit and destroy his writing. As some reviews in the Indian press have already noted, the book is neither written to provide a catalogue of horrors nor to ask for sympathy (Farooqui 2019). Its almost dispassionate style manages to tell us something very important about the erosion of demo-cratic rights for minorities and the particular dispositif of the Indian state as it is deployed in prisons, which is not available in the abstract reflections on the nature of justice or cruelty. I read this book as showing how the apparatus of anti-terror legislation has very little to do with control of terrorism and everything to do with the targeting of the Muslim minority – testimony to how cruelty hides under the veil of legality and the govern-ance of security regarding both the constitution of the social and what we understand to be human forms of life.

The first point that strikes one in the book *Begunah Qaidi* is that it is addressed to a specific kind of reader. Though initially it seems that the reader belongs to a general reading public, there is a slow shift that hap-pens so that in the end it becomes a pedagogy for young Muslim men who might end up being caught in the net of the police under the terror-related laws, and end up in special courts such as the MCOCA court. Here is what Wahid Shaikh writes:

> Though innocent, when we were caught by the police in the bomb blast case of 7/11 we could not understand for many days as to what was happening to us. We were think-ing that the police had mistakenly arrested us and we will be released soon. But with the passage of time this belief turned out to be false. . . . I began to realize then that if every person in Muslim society was aware of the earlier cases of bomb blasts he would have been helped by know-

ing these things. I mean he could have moved his hands and feet to protect himself. It was for this reason that I held the thought in my heart that, there was a need to give a detailed account of how we were ensnared in the 7/11 case and it was necessary to make the people (*janta*) aware so that it must not transpire that if in future the police trap an innocent person in a bomb blast case, he is unprepared mentally to face the police in court.[7]

Even in this opening paragraph there is a shift between a generic public (*janta*), Muslim society (Muslim *samaj*), and a future in which the same event may repeat itself with a different Muslim young man who will need not just general awareness that torture is routinely practiced in Indian prisons but also specifics on how the police talk, what enticements they might offer, which forms of torture will they use, and how you should be dealing with, say, physical beatings, humiliations, narco-analysis tests, substances injected into your anus to create unbearable burning sensations. From the general to the particular, the idea is not to shock the reader but to give a cool, collected account of how each of these methods comes to be inserted into different moments of a long unfolding of the way the police build up a case. It takes a while for these prisoners to realize that what they took to be a "mistake" was indicative of a different kind of truth – namely, that they are merely scapegoats in the game in which the police have to produce suspects, and nail the evidence in order to convert these so-called suspects into the accused and then into convicted criminals to cover up their failures in locating who the real culprits in particular cases are.

Some years ago, I wrote about my general understanding of these issues based upon my close friendship with a police officer in Amritsar who was an upright police officer working in the anti-terror squad. He educated me on the ways in which the political process in militancy and insurgency cases works through police practices before he was himself shot dead by one of his own subordinates (see Das 2007). I had also learnt much about the way police diaries are produced, the refusals to file First Information Reports in police stations and the whole scene of bribery, of police informers, of the connections between local dons and the police on the basis of my present work in urban slums (see Das 2019a). However, I had not been able to work out how scale comes to matter when cases that exist at the level of poor neighborhoods become resources for the police to anchor small events at neighborhood levels to scenes of national catastrophes such as the bomb blasts in cities in order to produce suspects and convert them into high-level criminals. And further, how specific forms of intimidation that prisoners face while waiting for their cases to come up become part of the standard procedures through which police devise investigative techniques that will show them to be diligent and active as they cover up the lack of any systematic information on which they are supposed to be acting. In the case of the 1993 bomb blasts, I was able to find documents that helped me decipher how the number of people arrested went up from dozens to hundreds as the main culprits managed to evade arrest for a long time. This is what Mr. B, the defense lawyer, was referring to when he spoke of the nexus among police, politicians, and leaders of underground crime syndicates.

Wahid Shaikh's book is structured in a masterful plot line. Organized in six chapters, each chapter highlights a particular technique or police procedure with a compelling analytical point. We learn of every step in the procedures actually followed by the police (not simply prescribed in police manuals): the way police first prepare the false case, contact family members and friends, craft a story in which they can prepare false witnesses, and keep up a constant harassment, creating an atmosphere of fear around the accused. There is an attrition of the everyday life of the suspect as he is not immediately put under arrest but has to report every day to the police station (as described above) where he might be interrogated repeatedly, sometimes accompanied by beatings and threatened with arrest if he reveals what is actually transpiring. In this period, the police also harass his relatives with phone calls, visits, threats, and inducements to provide witness against the suspect. Next, after he is arrested, he is left completely in the dark about what the charges are; nor are the legal provisions requiring that the accused be provided with a lawyer or informing his relatives of his arrest followed till a few days have passed. Through the use of first-degree torture (which will subsequently move into second- and third-degree torture), the suspect is repeatedly compelled toward signing false confessions. By the time he is produced before a magistrate (after anything from 14 days to a month), he is warned of more severe torture if he dares to complain before the magistrate of any pressure from the police. This analysis is buttressed by short biographies of the 12 accused in the Mumbai train blast case followed by the accounts of the witnesses for the defense. A subsequent chapter on torture is openly pedagogic, telling prisoners what to do or not do. For instance, when being beaten one should try to position one's body in relation to the thrashing belt in such a way that maximum bruises are left on the body; to overcome the normal reaction of avoiding the blows; and to then show these bruises in court and ask for medical examination. It is not that this strategy will succeed in court, writes Wahid Shaikh, but neither will the strategy of concealing the facts of torture be of any use in getting released from prison.[8] The final chapter provides a comparison between different bomb blast cases.

The contradictions Shaikh shows in the police accounts are blatant, and though courts have released many accused because of the obviously forced confessions and contradictions in the stories of "recovery" of material produced in evidence, the blatant injustice and the negligence of the judiciary to recognize facts of torture in prison during the long duration in which cases are being tried, are striking. It is part of the security apparatus developed by the state that there is no jurisprudence on compensation to victims under the terror laws for police brutality and miscarriage of justice, mainly due to the immunity granted to government officials against prosecution without previous permission of the government.

It is not only the content of the text that is compelling; it is also the narrative techniques. The grammatical devices in the text such as the juxtaposition of the habitual past tense, which shows the relentless use of torture, with dated events that introduce frightening interruptions in the everyday, depict different rhythms and tempos though which the horror of the violence is communicated without once resorting to horrifying language which would allow a voyeuristic gaze on the bodies of the accused and the tortured. I will give just one example. Under the subheading "Third Degree Torture ka Silsila" – "The Ongoing Third Degree Torture," Wahid Shaikh writes:

> From September 13 to September 26, 2006, for 14 days I was kept locked up in the death chamber. During this period, different policemen would come, they would write my testimony, sometimes recording it on the computer. They would subject me to different modes of torture and again and again they would ask me to accept the story of (made up by) Raghuvamshi (the senior officer). And I would say again and again, I am innocent. The children of my school are suffering (because of my absence), I should be released ... They would show me different people's

photographs, and ask me if I could identify them. I do not know any of them. (p. 270)

Here the relentless repetition of torture, interrogation, testimony, torture, interrogation, testimony, etc., creates the sense of time as continuous. In contrast, the dated events are the punctuating points, showing which inspector came to get a signature, or on which date the accused was presented before a judge, or even the date on which the accused was released on bail. I don't think that Wahid Shaikh uses these temporal markers as literary devices and yet it is a stunning use of the properties of Hindi and Urdu to create a resonance between the experience and its expression. The orchestration of temporality in terms of surprise, anticipation, waiting, creation of hope, and its relentless thwarting is part of the anatomy of torture itself. Here are two examples.

The police would repeatedly call my brother and harass him that Wahid should be sent to such and such police station for interrogation ... 14 August when I was teaching the children in my school when the headmistress of the school called me to her office. I went from the classroom to her office where three police officers were present. The headmistress told me that these are three police officers who have come to take you for some inquiries. They introduced themselves as officials from Vijay Saliskar's office and their names are Alaknore, Dalvi, and Mayankar. They asked me, are you Wahid Sir? I said, "yes, what is the matter?" They said they are from the Crime Branch and the higher officials have called me and that I will be released after a short time. The headmistress said that, "Wahid Sir is a very good teacher, we have no complaints against him. He cannot be involved in any destructive (violent) acts." They said this is just for routine questioning.[9] I told my colleagues that they are not going to release me soon – the police is not so upright (*sharif*). I ask you just to inform my relative Mahmood Azim that the police has taken me for interrogation. Mahmood used to work at that time close to my school in an office. Then I got ready and came down from the school where a private car of the police men was parked. As soon as they made me sit in the car, they started hitting me and started cursing and abusing me. I was taken aback by their behavior. Then continuously barking insults at me, they took me to the vicinity of Byculla Railway Station (Western) to the office of DCP (Deputy Commissioner of Police), Railway. There they beat me mercilessly, tortured me and shut me in lockup. (pp. 262–3)

What this lengthy quotation shows is the shifts in tenses. Wahid starts with a continuous past referring to the ongoing harassment of his brother, then shifts to the use of the definite past tense, when a date is given (August 14). The headmistress is anticipating the interrogation and offering testimony on Wahid's behalf, unprompted though. She uses the word *vidhvansak* (destructive, violence), though the shadow of the word terrorist is lurking in the shadows. Wahid shifts to a habitual present, where the long-term experience of policing in his neighborhood is expressed – "the police are not so upright." There is a further marking of time by the honorifics used in the headmistress's office – "Are you Wahid *Sir?* – and the deluge of abuses and vulgarities that follow in the car and the police station. There are other descriptions Wahid gives of the way in which trust in words is destroyed. He recalls a visit from his brother who had been informed that Wahid would soon be released, the policeman telling them that the paperwork might take a little time, and then using that moment of hope to suddenly drag him into a room where he is brutally beaten or tortured.

Bringing Social Theory into the
Scene of the Inhuman

Reading a book that takes such a clear-eyed view on cruelty, one might be forgiven in thinking that what Wahid Shaikh depicts is the scene of the inhuman; indeed, the very vocabulary in human rights that speaks of "cruel and inhuman punishment" makes us think that there is some kind of fall from the human into a different domain – that of the inhuman. Recent writing in anthropology abhors the attention given to horror, cruelty, and even suffering, on the grounds that it ignores the resources for the "good" that all societies possess (Ortner 2016; Robbins 2013, 2016). Recently a reviewer commented on my depiction of the legal trajectory in a case in which an eight-year-old child in one of the neighborhoods I work in was kidnapped and brutally raped and tortured (see Das 2020: ch. 8). The reviewer commented that there was nothing to explain in that story, because the case was clearly that of a "psychopath." I think Wahid Shaikh's book is a challenge to such a view in the most compelling terms because the evidence of the social in these scenes of torture is everywhere. If the police and army personnel use torture in relation to suspected terror cases or in subjugating the "enemy," it is not because they are psychopaths who have fallen into inhumanity but because such procedures have become part of standard operating procedures and their depictions in film and television serials and secretly recorded videos seep into the lives of many people. Because Wahid Shaikh's eye is so focused on what is going on around him (an enormous accomplishment, indeed), we see how forms of talk in the scenes of torture are anchored into everyday understandings of what is an insult, the bruises caused by humor directed at victims in such contexts, and, I add, the challenge of how we might restore the world by giving back an integrity to things so they might learn what is their own nature. I leave the expansion of these points for another occasion, but briefly mention how the omens and premonitions of the destruction of the social fabric and of relations with things years after the physical torture is over is everywhere in the text.

First, objects are displaced from their normal functions. One such object is the rubber belt (*patta*) usually placed on wheat grinding machines in India, which, when used to thrash someone, makes a horrifying sound as it hits bodies but leaves no visible marks. That this instrument is transformed in the police station is shown in the inscriptions in Hindi, which Wahid Shaikh reports, that are marked on every *patta* hanging on walls of police stations. Examples are, "Hear my voice" (*meri aavaz suno*), "Law is blind" (*andha kanoon*), etc., which are references to what is happening or will happen to the man in their custody now, but also refers to titles of popular Hindi films. The terrifying humor is produced through the condensation of different registers of the social and the natural, both distorted and stretched out of shape and context. Austin (2016) argued that the use of everyday objects for torture is because very often torture takes place in topologically displaced locations or in the context of wider warfare. However, as we have seen, in India torture takes place within ordinary police stations where the presence of such objects as the *patta* makes the possibility of brutal beating ever present: or, in the case of terror trials when torture is used to extract confessions, the social embedding of the person being tortured is evident in the various ways kin and neighbors are brought into the network of those who will be harassed and pressurised to give evidence. In these contexts, the use of everyday objects extends the scene of torture even when the accused has been released because he cannot obliterate these objects from his everyday life, nor can he simply live with the betrayals that he cannot easily forget. This is the difficulty of reality where the nature of bitter compromises poses problems for thought, but much more for the very project of bringing life back into living.

Second, forms of talk, even in the frightening scenario of the police station, draw from forms of life where words condense in themselves bits of ritual, mythology, and history, which constitute their physiognomy. For instance, the main investigating officer in Wahid Shaikh's case was a man named Raghuvanshi, which literally means one from the lineage of Raghu, the ancestor of the revered god-king Rama. At one point as he was offering inducements to Wahid Shaikh, Raghuvanshi reportedly said, the torture will stop, all cases against you will be withdrawn, and we will rehabilitate you completely – you know, you can believe me – "I am after all, a Raghuvanshi." The reference is to the famous couplet in the *Ramacharitamanasa*, the devotional text in Avadhi written by Tulasidas, the medieval poet, in which Rama says, "*Raghukul rita sada chali aayi – prana jaaye par vachan na jayi*" ["The tradition of the lineage of Raghu is uninterrupted, life might be drained out of you, but the word is not betrayed"]. This couplet circulates as a devotional song recorded on popular cassettes, on YouTube, and is the title of a Hindi film. In this context, the statement bristles with violence, for the promise might be fulfilled in many ways. It might very well allude to Muslims being coerced into saying "*Jay Sri Rama*," "victory to Lord Rama" by lynching crowds, much as religious slogans shouted during riots take on an ominous character.

Finally, here is a passage from the chapter on torture in which a prisoner is encouraged to see differently the practice of making him naked and humiliating him.

Remember, you have not become naked out of your own will. You have not become naked to commit any dirty or obscene act. You have been *made* naked for the only reason that you must agree to the false story being crafted by the police. For the duration in which the police keeps you without clothes (*belibas*) do not curse yourself. ... Bear with it. For this Allah will reward you, because you are enduring all this for the sake of truth. (Shaikh 2017: 370, my translation)

If Wahid Shaikh is able to show some mastery over the experience of torture, it is not that he is somehow healed, but that the impulse to not let his experience disappear is simultaneously steeped in a cultural imaginary (say, that of Allah watching what is happening to you) and an attempt to convert a form of shaming that comes from the experience of the human (an animal would not be humiliated by a lack of clothes) to another register in which the mark of humiliation is to be converted into a sign of not giving up. But torture does not affect individual bodies alone and this is a lesson the police officers know well.

At no point in Wahid Shaikh's writing does one get a sense that we are dealing with "bare life." The enormous influence of Agamben's (1998) formulation of bare life must mean that it spoke to some regions of biopolitical life for analyzing our contemporary concerns that held great appeal. As is well known, for Agamben the figure of *homo sacer* holds the key to an understanding of sovereignty and modern political and legal codes because of what it reveals about a sovereign's power to resort to a boundless state of exception. The figure of *homo sacer*, Agamben suggests, is both outside divine law and outside human law, a thought that crystallizes in his signature expression that "homo sacer can be killed but not sacrificed." I will not repeat here the many discussions on historical accuracy of the different figures

Agamben evokes touching on such questions as whether the father's right to kill his son, the stateless refugee who can be killed because he cannot claim citizenship of any state, or the inhabitants of Nazi camps reduced to bare survival, can be collapsed into a single figure. What interests me here is a different question. If the quality of being bare is simply the question of having been stripped of the positive attributes of citizenship, and is to be defined only by exclusion, then it emerges as primarily a negative category. But as philosophers of the negative from Nagarjuna to Heidegger tell us, what is negative cannot be simply defined as a lack as if something which *was* is now *not*.[10] Agamben himself alludes to these vexing questions, citing Heidegger that the ontological meaning of the notness (*Nichtkeit*) of existential negativity remains obscure (Agamben 1991: 3). Yet, when it comes to bare life, he seems to be content in thinking of bare as a negation defined by a lack alone. All this would be purely speculative if it did not run against what Wahid Shaikh shows in his book, with examples, of which there are many, exhorting the use of ritual formulae, of seeing nakedness not as shaming the victim but shaming the perpetrator, to block the torturer's victory over the mind of the victim.

The entire vocabulary, gestures, embedded references to films, songs, sacred texts, kin, and neighbors shows the thick sociality, the criteria drawn from within forms of life through which suspects are located, witnesses procured, evidence collated, and within which torture unfolds as a practice. Think of the fact that it was Wahid Shaikh's wife's brother who was coerced into first giving false testimony against him to the effect that he had harbored Pakistani terrorists in his apartment; and that it was the courage his brother-in-law displayed in court that led to Wahid's acquittal. But many are beaten down into submission and end up giving testimonies against their own relatives and friends. My great fear is that democracy cannot be sustained if these practices become generalized and the possibility of intimacy in everyday life itself becomes corroded as the excellent work of Verdery (2018) shows for Romania. What the anti-terror law creates is not only individuals broken down and shattered, but also families, relatives, and communities that are coerced into becoming inadvertent subjects of the law and liars and betrayers of kin, family, lovers, friends. The philosopher Stanley Cavell memorably wrote, "And isn't it the case that not the human horrifies me, but the inhuman, the monstrous? Very well. But only what is human can be inhuman. – Can only the human be monstrous? If something is monstrous and we do not believe that there are monsters, then only the human is the candidate for the monstrous" (Cavell 1979: 418). Wahid Shaikh challenges us to come up not with a definition or a boundary of what is human but to chart the routes through which the career of the human and its affinity with the inhuman might be traced in the experiences and the resulting damning critique of Indian democracy he has provided.

Yet Another Register of Knowing

If Wahid Shaikh's writing is transformative because he is able to carry his overwhelming knowledge and to transform it into a scene of instruction, it is harder to capture the sense of menace that stalks inhabitants of Muslim neighborhoods, in which arbitrary arrests have taken place and in which there is a growing sense that violence is not temporally bounded (as in riots) but could erupt anytime and anywhere. One of the issues that came up in the consideration of cases tried in TADA, POTA, or MCOCA courts is the question of jurisdiction – how judicial reasoning tried to distinguish between ordinary crime and terror that would threaten the sovereignty of the country.[11]

As we saw, this distinction is constantly elided in police procedures in which confessions elicited in the course of one trial can be seamlessly used to trap someone else. To my surprise, I found that a similar anxiety on how ordinary transgressions might spill into an extraordinary spiral of punishment and death pervades everyday life in Muslim neighborhoods now. In providing the following scene I show an anxiety which is not about separating the good and the bad, but touches on a different register of ethics, one that is forged in relation to the difficulty of maintaining any integrity in one's ongoing relationships.

One of the men in this neighborhood is a great entertainer as he can spin stories and songs from all kinds of quotidian experiences. However, many neighbors fear that he lacks tact and that he has a loose tongue. On my last visit to Delhi, he confided in me that he was very scared of the fact that the kinds of everyday transgressions that were contained earlier but spill into major Hindu–Muslim confrontations now might have become lethal. He gave me the example of how his Hindu friends would sometimes tease him and say — *yahan ke bashinde ho, hamara hi khate ho aur hmko hi galiyan dete ho* – you live here, you eat our food and still you curse us? I could respond then and say "oh, yes, you are just lower caste men – I am a descendant of a Rajput – so what if a foolish ancestor became a Muslim" and he bursts into peals of laughter.

> But now my son tells me I should control my tongue. I fear that one day when maybe I have annoyed Allah by taking a drink or two, and I am sneaking back home in the dark, some group of righteous Muslims will catch hold of me and ask me – "You are so close to the Hindus – now say Jai Shri Ram?"[12] Then I will know that if I say it, I am

doomed because they will accuse me of insulting Allah, and if I don't say it, I am doomed because they will accuse me of hypocrisy.

I was stunned by all the inversions he had managed to concoct. Every day newspapers were reporting about lynching of Muslim men suspected of eating beef; every day there were reports of Hindu men catching hold of a Muslim-looking stranger, and asking him to recite – Jai Shri Rama – and threatening or even killing the helpless man regardless of whether he recited the slogan or refused to do so. Was Aziz *bhai* now telling me that inverted veiled languages were the only ones that were left between us – we, who had been such good friends?

And in a short chat with the brother of another accused in the bomb blast case who told me "It is easier for those terrorists or martyrs who died – but for those who are, may be quite worthless like me, who would not have the courage to stand up to torture, it is a numbing fear that given the circumstances you will give out names, even if the ones who bear those names have done nothing."

It is not only what is happening in courts but also how the spaces of intimacy have been darkened that constitute the texture of inordinate knowledge – overwhelming knowledge borne with fortitude or with the desire to flee, but always more than simply archived or bare knowledge.

3
The Dispersed Body of the Police and Fictions of the Law

In the last chapter, we looked closely at the working of terror laws promulgated to deal with presumed threats to the "sovereignty and territorial integrity" of India. In this context, I examined a variety of documents that held traces within them of police manipulation, forgeries, made-up events, intimidation to coerce witnesses to extract false confessions from them. In this chapter, I want to pose two questions that I hope to take forward by a shift of place to the communities from which legal cases arise and in which the apparatus of the state becomes enfolded (see Das and Poole 2004). First, how do we understand the fact that violence is to be found *within* the law? Although it would be tempting to frame the relation between law and violence in terms of the dichotomy of founding violence and maintaining violence as Benjamin (2019 [1978]) held, I suggest that there are other ways of looking at the issue that do not take the characteristics of sovereign power too much for granted. We already saw in the Introduction that alternative genealogies of sovereignty, such as those contained in the figures of Vedic Gods or in the figuration of different aspects of the warrior function in the

Mahabharata, showed not only the force considered legitimate for the sovereign but also the rogue element of sovereignty crystallized through the figure of Indra. How might we then think of the close proximity of law and force/violence that comes to the surface sometimes openly, sometimes hidden in the recesses of police procedures, and court judgments?

The second question I pursue pertains to the manner in which judicial truth is made dependent on fictions produced within the law. We saw something of this fictional quality in the way in which the different plot points revealed themselves in confessions by the accused that clearly bore the signature of having been crafted to fit a particular story of conspiracy. The scattering of words in the original documents that were in Hindi or Marathi – words that have a Sanskritic physiognomy, such as *pramana, uddeshya, prakriya*, rather than the more Urdu and English inflected popular Hindi (*subut, maksad, procedure*) left tell-tale signs of manufactured documents. Similarly, the fact that the same spelling errors or errors in syntax were found in the police affidavits pointed to a common document from which all affidavits were copied though they were supposed to be singular responses that could calculate the risks that different accused persons posed if, say, released on bail. Can we then think of fictions of the law not in opposition to its truth but rather as a kind of double that hides within the factual language but leaves tell-tale signs? Toward the end of this chapter, I will return to the question of the relation between fiction and lies and trace the different ways one would address this issue depending on whether it is the jurist who is asking the question or someone who is seeking the protection of the law, as well as someone who is seeking protection *from* the law?

I submit that these two features residing within sovereign power – the intimacy of law and violence and the coupling of judicial truth with legal fictions – reveal aspects of policing and of the legal mechanisms that do not remain confined within police stations, and courts of law, but spill into everyday life, into the slum acts that I seek to describe here. This aspect of policing is what I call the dispersed body of the police.

It is time I took the reader to one of the neighborhoods where I follow a case of abduction and show the working of ordinary police practices through a close look at a trial that did not come under any terror laws but which demonstrated the role of small tools of knowledge (memos, police diary, spot report)[1] in a normal trial as well as how legal fictions function with regard to the singularity of a case.

Ordinary Violence and Legal Fictions

In the month of April 2011, an eight-year-old girl child living in one of my field sites, a shanty settlement in Noida in the national capital region (Delhi), was abducted, forcibly restrained, tortured, and raped till she was rescued four months later under somewhat mysterious circumstances.[2] The case was adjudicated in a District Sessions Court in which the accused, a neighbor, and his two accomplices (his present wife and his ex-wife) were found to be guilty of wrongful confinement, aggravated rape and attempted murder (*Government of India* v. *Sudhanshu and Others* [2011]). The main accused was sentenced to life imprisonment without possibility of parole. The two women were each sentenced to seven years of rigorous imprisonment with labor. When I considered the legal judgment in terms of its narrative structure and the place of detail in that structure, I was struck by the ubiquity of legal fictions, not only in the technical juridical sense but in the intimacy they established between law and everyday life of policing (see Das 2019a).

It is well known that the production of facts in the course of court trials entails fictions that are not simply added to facts but are produced by the law itself. Many scholars recognize that legal definitions of persons or objects can go against our quotidian experience by creating equivalences that violate our ordinary realism around things and persons – for example, pigeons could be defined as predatory birds (Latour 2010), or runaway slaves treated as animals for purposes of the law. In the last chapter I looked at one set of documents that were prepared by higher level officials; in this chapter I will look at documents that are produced in a routine way such as the "police diary," or the "spot report" at the lower echelons of the police hierarchy, and try to see not only the plot but also the characters such as "police informer," and "police witness," which are recognizable to the law as shown in references made to them in legal judgments as well as in their routine appearance in police diaries and affidavits produced before the courts. The role play, however, is outside formal police procedures. The discourses and practices around these characters make it necessary to relate what goes on *inside* the courtroom to what goes on *outside* the courtroom – the matter is not simply that of expanding the context in order to flesh out in more detail the lives of the characters recognizable to the law, but of realizing that the truths established in courts entail projections through which the outside and the inside are joined by loose stitches. Sometimes these projections follow a natural movement and at other times the direction is turned away from the natural course. The term natural is used here to suggest that a form of life entails the mutual absorption of the natural and the social. Thus, when I say that a projection might follow a natural movement, I do not mean to suggest that the direction of this movement is predetermined, but rather that there is a feeling of rightness about it: it can be placed as occurring within a form of life. Sandra Laugier demonstrates this feeling of rightness with an example from Austin's (1962) famous essay on excuses. Laugier writes:

> Austin points out that we do not give just any type of excuse for just any type of action. One can excuse lighting a cigarette or covering one's books by 'the force of habit', but a killer cannot invoke the force of habit to excuse his murdering. (2018: 133)

The reason the murderer's excuse that he kills out of habit is experienced as wacky (maybe he is mad) is that the word habit does not quite belong here; one can imagine ritual murders or the murders committed by a serial killer and think how a clever lawyer might use them as excuses in a cultural defense argument or in an insanity plea; but if someone were to say it is my habit to kill, the sentence does not seem to have been spoken within a human form of life. Something seems wrong in how such a speaker uses language. So, while projecting a word in a new context tells us the limits of the word, this limit is not settled in advance. Courts, of course, try hard to iron out the fierce ambiguity of language in everyday life, but what they do is end up introducing new kinds of ambiguities which are erased through fiat rather than through testing the limits of how far and in which direction a word might be projected. For instance, the sprinkling of Sanskrit words purportedly citing the speech of an accused who is an Urdu speaker in what are claimed to be voluntary confessions raises a suspicion; it does not seem quite right. Why does it fail to raise an alert for the presiding judge? The reason seems to be that the language of official documents is already assumed to be distant from everyday speech, and this fact itself assumes certain police practices to be a part of the everyday life of law.[3]

The room for improvisation and play with how an outside might be brought into the inside of a court accounts for the paradox that falsity in court may become the means for producing both justice and injustice in the course of a trial. Of course, this "outside" has to be defined on a case-by-case basis, giving rise to a multiplicity of contexts within which any single "case" unfolds. As an example, Sehdev (2018) shows that this outside could well be the movements of litigants in the several spaces in and around the court where the unstable relation between the sensory and the forensic renders allegations against women simultaneously forceful and fragile in cases of domestic disputes. But this outside might also be constituted in temporal terms – as covering the entire institutional landscape – that are implicated in either moving a case forward or scuttling it at the neighborhood level. The networks of connections between a case and its outside proliferate in different directions and it will require patient deciphering of detail to show how filling out a context might also make us see the characters of these legal stories in very different lights.

The Policing Apparatus

In order to decipher how a particular dispositif of the state is made present in these neighborhoods, let us first see how references to the police appear in the adjudication process in the case mentioned above (*Government of India* v. *Sudhanshu and Others* [2011]). I will refer to the victim as Kh, as she appears in the legal judgment although other records, including the medical forensic reports, mention her by her full name. When Kh had failed to return home after having gone out to play on that fateful night of April 2011, her parents had first tried to trace her whereabouts themselves but they had failed to find her. The next day they had gone to the police outpost in the locality and tried to file a missing person report, but for months the police officer on duty had refused to register their complaint. Not only had the police officer reportedly asked for a bribe, he had also threatened that they were trying to ensnare innocent people by making false accusations against them and that their daughter had not been abducted as they claimed, but had run away with someone. For nearly three months there were no efforts on the part of the police to trace the girl. In this period, while forcibly restrained in a small room by the man who had abducted her, she had endured repeated sexual assaults, rape, and torture.[4] In an earlier account of this incident, I provided a detailed description of the contingent events through which this case was propelled into public attention and thus reached the courts. But in the interim, the parents were unable to get any help at all and even the victim's father had given up, leaving his wife with the entire burden of trying to find ways to trace their daughter. We can get a sense of the utter frustration and the atmosphere of fear and intimidation that the mother faced in pursuing her efforts to find her daughter and to get a missing person case registered through the various petitions she submitted to higher level officials and to elected representatives in high positions. The last such petition entitled, "*Requesting legal action in a case of filing of wrong FIR and negligence in investigation of missing person,*" submitted by the victim's mother, with the help of a local branch of an NGO that she had finally been able to muster support from, stated:

> All kinds of allegations that are not fit to be repeated are laid against anyone who tries to help me. As a result, far from coming forward to help me, no one is willing to even

talk to me. When I go to the police post to inquire about the case at least two people unknown to me follow me. For the past one month, I have gone and cried and lamented at the police post (*rota bilakhta raha*)[5] but the police there have not even written a report – acting on the case is miles away. Sir, the main point is that my daughter has been missing from somewhere near my house since 9 p.m. on 30.4.2011, but in connivance with the criminals and in order to save them, it has been written in the police report that she was missing from school. (Original in Hindi, my translation)

In the course of the court trial, accounts of the delays and intimidation that the parents had been submitted to did not surface at all. In fact, there remains some confusion as to whether the girl had managed to escape even though grievously injured, and was rescued when some people in a nearby market noticed her and caught her abductor as he was chasing her (some media reports had claimed this but she denied it in court); or, whether she was "recovered" by the diligent efforts of the police officer with the help of a police informer, as appeared in the court documents. The one thing that is certain is that because of the concurrence of certain larger events such as the local-level mobilization of a nation-wide anti-corruption movement that was at the height of its power at that time, and because of coming assembly elections, local-level protests on various matters had emerged and grown in intensity. This specific milieu at that specific time made the case of Kh come into the national media and led to the involvement of the Human Rights Commission in the case. There were also hints of the possibility in the media that this case was part of the larger scene of trafficking for which sporadic evidence surfaced in the neighborhood from time to time. Clearly within the neighborhood there was more than one story that was circulated – for instance, some said that the policeman who had initially refused to register the case had come and begged Kh's mother to save him by not bringing any complaint about the delay in registering the case; others said that he had bribed the family to agree to tell the story that emerged later in court because it would lead to both the culprit being punished and save him from being dismissed. Without setting ourselves as the arbiters of which story is the true one, let us instead turn to the scene in the courtroom and the way the police procedures come to find expression in the judgment. I zoom in to the moments when the judge is commenting on the significance of the evidence given by the police officer.

After having established that the girl had clearly not been coached to give false witness as suggested, somewhat lamely, by the defense (her severe injuries were proof enough to the contrary), the judge came to the "decisive" proof established by the investigation conducted by the police officer, and referred to the *roznamcha* (daily diary) maintained by him. In the words of the presiding judge, "Although this witness (the police officer) is giving evidence in his formal capacity – *yadyapi yeh sakshi aupcharik sakshi hai* – in the present circumstances his testimony is very important because it is through him that the victim has been recovered and the accused have been arrested red handed" (lit. *mauko par giraftar kiyu gaya*, arrested at the site or moment of the crime).

The judge noted that the witness (i.e., the investigating officer) had clearly stated that on being informed by a police informer, he had taken the informer (duly disguised in a face mask) and, accompanied by two female police officers and two independent witnesses, they had gone to a nearby village to a house that the informer directed them toward. The police diary contained detailed descriptions of how the girl was recovered from this house.

According to this account, when all other leads had gone cold, the investigating officer learnt from a *mukhavir* (police informer) that the victim had been abducted by Sudhanshu and his two wives and was being forcibly restrained in a room that they had rented in a nearby area. (There is no record in the police diary as to how the informer learnt about this, or when. The usual form of reporting in police diaries and police affidavits that we examined in the last chapter is simply to say that the police had learnt this from a reliable source.) However, the judge summarizes the actions of the investigating officer as follows: "Accompanied by the said police informer, two female police officers and two witnesses from the nearby market, the investigating officer had gone to the area where the *mukhavir* pointed out the house and then left. The officer was able to forcibly enter the house where they found the victim crouched in a corner with deep injuries". The poignant moments of this discovery are related in the exact words of the policeman: "When she saw her parents, she ran to her mother and cried pitiably while hugging her." We learn from the judge's summary that a recovery report memo was prepared on the spot in the presence of the parents, and the original was signed by the two accompanying female officers, the two independent witnesses and the parents. The memo and the police diary had been submitted as exhibits in the court (*Government of India* v. *Sudhanshu and Others* [2011], my translation).

I will leave for now the question of how the genre of storytelling in court partakes of bits of melodrama in order for the testimony to be considered "reliable." Note that the reliability in question is less of the victim's words since the forensic report had already given a graphic account of the injuries to the vagina, the severed tongue, the bleeding wounds, the cigarette burns;

it is more about establishing the *reliability of the police officer* whose negligence and intimidation *outside* the courtroom is converted into sincerity and diligence in the pursuit of his duties by what transpires *inside* the courtroom.

The family, nevertheless, found considerable relief in the judgment that led to life imprisonment imposed on the accused with no provision for parole, and thus removed the dangers posed by this man and his wives to the safety of the girl and her family. However, the judgment also had the effect of transforming a police officer known in the neighborhood to be at the nexus of various incidents of intimidation into an honest and hard-working police officer who was reinstated in his job (albeit transferred to another area) after a departmental inquiry. If the scene of recovery recorded in the police diary has the feel of something rehearsed, I should mention that many people in the neighborhood can point to the fact that the police always conveniently find the same people repeatedly to act as "independent witnesses" when "recoveries" are made, and it is common knowledge in the area that the police diary will contain empty pages that can be filled out as need arises. If asked how they know these rumors to be true, people will hesitate to point to specific police officers, or to specific cases in the neighborhood for fear of retaliation. However, various Bollywood films that had exposed these practices in high-profile murder cases were readily cited as evidence of these police practices. The staging of the characters, such as *mukhavirs* (police informer) and "independent" witnesses who serve the interests of the police in this manner as upright citizens in courts, conceals from view the different kinds of dangers that these characters pose when they return to the ordinary lives in the neighborhoods in which they live and work. In order to take these issues further, we will need to briefly consider the actual police procedures followed in these neighborhoods.

The Dispersed Body of the Police

It is not easy to ascertain definite information on the *mukhavir* in this case, as in many other cases. In the case of Kh, when the prosecutor was challenged to produce the police informer in court, the judge herself stated that police informers were part of the police procedures and it was imperative to protect their anonymity because the police depended upon information gathered from them. Yet a lot is known in the neighborhood about how the police use information they collect in both small skirmishes and disputes and large cases that come to involve suspicions of some big event such as transnational trafficking rings or suspicions of harboring "terrorists." Despite knowing a lot about Kh and her family, I have not tried to probe into the suspicions reported in some newspapers that Kh's abduction might have been part of the rampant incidents of child trafficking in which young girls are lured into predatory relationships and circulated in markets of sex, because it is not easy to establish the sources of such news. Instead, I have taken the very texture of indefiniteness as crucial to understanding the place of such figures in the everyday life of the neighborhood.

It is widely known in the neighborhoods I work in that local-level police posts are not places to turn to for one's own protection. Therefore, people in the neighborhood who are seen to be in easy familiarity with the lower-level policemen are viewed with suspicion. From my conversations with people in these areas about safety, intimidation, as well as resources needed to protect oneself from the clutches of the law, I deciphered four "characters" that repeatedly surfaced in these discussions. These were, respectively, the *mukhavir*, the local don, and the *bhu* mafia on one side as people to be wary of; and the political intermediary, who might be a *jaankar* (knowledgeable person) or a political lackey who hangs around aspiring leaders to do their work, to whom one could turn for help, on the other side. One figure who could appear within any of these formations was a certain kind of woman who was seen to be somewhat loosely tied to the bonds of domestic life in that such women lived with their families but were not too constrained by domesticity and respectability. Before I describe more fully the atmosphere within which these figures come to life and how their kind of work finds expression in the local life of the neighborhoods, I want to clarify what I mean by the dispersed body of the police.

In fleshing out his idea that "power is never something that someone possesses, any more than it emanates from someone," Foucault, in his lectures on psychiatric power, takes us to the scene of the asylum (Foucault 2006: 4–5). Here, in the asylum, we find that:

> There is, then, a whole series of relays around the doctor ... First of all there are the supervisors ... (performing) the task of informing on the patients, of being the unarmed, inexpert gaze, the kind of optical canal through which the learned gaze, that is to say the objective gaze of the psychiatrist himself, will be exercised. This relayed gaze, ensured by the supervisors, must also take in the servants, that is to say those who hold the last link in the chain of authority ... Actually, the servant is the last relay of this network, of this difference in potential that pervades the asylum on the basis of the doctor's power; he is therefore the power below. But he is not just below because he is at the bottom of the hierarchy; he is also below because he must be below the patient.

This particular observation of the relays that allow power to be realized in the dispersion, relays, and networks shows a temporary configuration of what psychiatric power looked like at this moment (in the early nineteenth century, 1817–30), before it became solidified through its alliance with the law in France. It is a story about the steps in the making of a discipline (psychiatry) that was fragile but was trying to find its footing in the rapidly changing norms of biomedicine with regards to standards of evidence in establishing diagnoses. What interests me here is Foucault's notions about differences of potential that such a picture of power allowed to emerge. As the psychiatrist in Foucault's account moves from the asylum to the courtroom, his role changes as a different potential of the situation is realized. In the asylum Foucault speaks of the "formidable medical surplus power" (p. 269) because the doctor and the disciplinary system ultimately form a single body; but there is also the surplus power of the patient for it is the patient who will, in the final analysis, establish whether the psychiatrist is a mere disciplinarian or a doctor (p. 219). As the scene of psychiatry moves from the centrality of the asylum to the centrality of the court, and as patients suffer not so much from royal deliriums but the deliriums of the humble servants in themselves, the psychiatrist is recast as one who becomes the guardian of the social body, providing means for distinguishing between what is a crime and what is a disease. And here we come to a roadblock in our analogy between the dispersed body of the psychiatrist in the tokens and personnel of the asylum, and the dispersed body of the police in the neighborhood. If the dispersed body of the police forms a disciplinary dispositif, to the extent that it enables power to flow into the smallest capillary branches of the neighborhood, it is the small tools of knowledge, such as the police diary, which become the means of concealing from one part of the law (courts) the standard procedures of operation in another part of the law (the police).

Thinking of the police as part of a dispersed body changes somewhat how we think of communities within which surveillance mechanisms operate. Didier Fassin (2017), who has provided a compelling account of what he designates as the carceral condition in France, makes an interesting contrast between the texture of relations that characterize the interactions between the police and the people they come in contact with, and the way that guards in charge of prisons relate to the inmates. Noting that in France, "on average two police officers are killed in the line of duty every year, almost always by people involved in organized crime, while it is more than twenty years since a police guard has been killed by an inmate," Fassin postulates that some of this discrepancy might be traced to the everyday relations of distance and proximity between police and people on the one hand, and between guards and prisoners, on the other hand. It is worth citing Fassin more fully on this point:

> Second, with regard to their awareness of those they deal with, since the police know little if anything about the individuals they interact with, they can have a preconceived idea of them as criminals or even enemies thereby justifying their distant or aggressive attitude toward them; indeed they are usually incapable of distinguishing among their clientele because the only clues they have to interpret them are descriptions such as neighborhood, age, clothing, or skin color, which are the subject of unfavorable prejudices and lump together all those who present the same characteristics. Guards, by contrast, can go at least partially beyond these assumptions insofar as living among prisoners allows them to develop a degree of discernment. (p. 154)

Fassin's (2017) formulations might be correct in the case of police patrols that he has described with finesse, but if we expand the contexts in which police functions are distributed to reflect urban hierarchies, we get a different picture. In urban centers in India there are subtle distinctions and not so subtle distinctions between police placed in outposts in low-income areas; police officers working in stations located in more prestigious areas; and those who are put in charge of gathering evidence in high-profile cases of murder or serial bomb blasts – the perspective of the police on different rungs of the hierarchy might be quite different. These differences are not purely a matter of the more enlightened level of the elite rungs of police who might be expected to keep to the rule book, and the lower-level workers who break rules with impunity; it is rather that the kinds of sociality within which the police get enmeshed is determined by the tasks that fall on different kinds of police officers within these differentiated micro-geographies.[6] The point that I want to take forward, then, is to show how this dispersed body of the police secretes certain realities that function in one way at the level of low-income neighborhoods, and quite another way within police stations and torture rooms in which the police officers see themselves as being in charge of "national" security. At the level of neighborhoods and slums that are defined as crime-prone, the police use the police informers, the local dons, and the readily available mafia-like figures as their eyes, and their ears, and their hands. Such figures become points of danger for the residents of the neighborhood, but contentious disputes, and even more grievous events such as abductions and murders, are contained within the local milieus. On the other end are the hinges and junctions through which the small-time operators in these areas come to be violently conjoined to cases that propel them outside local societies. Information to lower-level police personnel that might lie inert for a long time comes alive through a version of eventalization as happens in riots, in the curbing of insurgencies, and in so-called terror-related cases. Let us first look at the texture of small events which reveal a particular face of policing at the level of neighborhoods before we turn to some big events more fully in this and the next chapter.

Navigating Everyday Dangers

The case of Kh had brought back memories and some discussions in the local media (small newspapers in Hindi that have limited circulation) about another notorious case known as the Nithari case, which happened in 2006, in the neighborhood where Kh lives. This was the case of serial killings in which skulls and bones of 17 victims were found in plastic bags in a drain in Nithari, an area within the larger Noida area. Of these victims, one was an adult woman but all the others were children. The case created a terrible scandal not only because the killers turned out to be a rich businessman and his man servant, but also because villagers accused the police of having ignored their complaints of disappeared children for nearly two years. Both the accused were ultimately found guilty and sentenced to death in 2017. In the locality where Kh lived, however, people were very reluctant to get involved in any discussions on cases of this sort. Instead of claiming to know anything definite, people in these neighborhoods resorted to indefinites. "You know that the *mahaul* (milieu) of this area is very bad," "you know that girls find it difficult to navigate alone here," "you know that we do not engage in anyone else's affairs," "we just engage with others as much as our work requires."[7] So, whatever the anger that had built up in 2006 (the Nithari case) or 2011 (Kh's case), it did not take long for it to dissipate completely. Yet people do use these indefinite forms of "knowing" when the need arises. I give a few short vignettes from my ethnography to show how the navigation of specific dangers requires people to know what resources they can marshal. And though uncertainty of outcomes is inherent in these navigations, these vignettes will, I hope, show the potentials contained in the network of police procedures in these neighborhoods.

Veeran, the Irrepressible

One of the women (I will call her Veeran) I came to know, it seemed to me, was always to be found sitting outside her house as one crossed the street into the main road. Sometimes she would be drying her hair in the sun, at other times she would be gossiping with some policeman from the police post located at the edge of the entrance to the neighborhood who had stopped by to take a break. She always hailed me with a friendly *"are madam kahan ka program hai aaj, zara idhar bhi darhsn deti jao* – so ma'am, what is the program for today, at least stop a moment and grace us with a glimpse." Veeran was actually notorious in the area as part of what the locals call the "bhu mafia" (i.e., land mafia). People will tell you that it is not possible to do any real estate transaction in the area without paying the "cut" she demands. Her husband is an alcoholic and she claims that all it takes to keep him quiet is a *thaili* (locally brewed alcohol illegally dispensed in plastic bags). Her two grown-up sons work in the house construction industry in the area. As I have explained elsewhere (Das 2014; Das and Walton 2015), there is an elaborate bureaucratic classification of localities that leads to minute administrative distinctions between "notified slums," "non-notified slums," "recognized colonies," "unapproved colonies," and so on. In fact, estimates suggest that about 60–70% of Delhi's population are living in these informal settlements. Even though the poor mostly live on such "occupied" land (Rao 2013), a combination of electoral politics and legal decisions have allowed these settlements to be regarded as permanent, and attempts to "regularize" such settlements on the part of local government are always under discussion. The point is that on one level there is continuous political activity in these areas as part of efforts to get claims over land, or water, or electricity secured. At another level, many of these areas have a reputation of being hubs of crime stemming precisely from the ambiguous status of ownership and insecurity built into land transactions. For instance, in an adjoining part of the neighborhood, ongoing feuding between two factions of a local *biradari* (collateral kin group) in one cluster of streets has led to murders, abduction, and exchange of threats that encompass in their ambit not only the kin groups but also the other residents even as they try not to take sides. The police *chauki* (outpost) that was supposed to be a temporary measure has now acquired a permanent presence in the area. Most of the time a group of policemen lounge around on string cots, although they are expected to make regular patrols of the area. I would often find them in some house or other drinking tea or having snacks. On one occasion, I found a very drunk policeman whom Veeran tried to chase away when she saw me. "What's happening?" I asked, and she replied, "*Do murder to pichle maheene mein ho gaye aur ek ladki bhaga li*" – "Two murders in the last month and one girl instigated to elope."

I know from casual conversations with various residents that they hold Veeran in contempt for the way she dresses (rarely does she wear the dupatta as it lies curled up on the cot on which she usually sits); or how she uses words like sister-fucker, mother-fucker, son of an owl, dog, born of a vagina, peppering her speech.

I have to admit though that she tried very hard not to fall into this pattern of speech in my presence. People in the neighborhood think she smokes and drinks, which is not uncommon for women from lower castes, but in these neighborhoods there have been significant efforts to earn greater respectability by putting restraints on women. One elderly Sikh told me that when they had added a new room on the first floor of their house, Veeran had turned up to demand her share and though they were able to bring her cut down a bit, they were in no position to refuse. "*Ji uske moonh nahin lagana chahte*" – lit. "we don't want to even touch her (speaking) mouth" – for it seems she could let loose strings of obscenities that would make you run for cover, once memorably having threatened to undress completely and shame everyone by appearing naked there and then if the family did not shell out the cash. "Why don't you report to the police?" I asked. "Oh, but it is from the police that she derives her power." So, it seemed that the police were part of the system of cuts, and would threaten anyone who would dare to take the matter further. I was surprised, then, to learn that Veeran had been the one to provide support and to resolve a contentious issue that had hit a family known to be a "*shareef*" or honest, gentle family.[8]

This was a family composed of a single mother with three daughters whose husband had abandoned her because she could not produce a son for him. At around the age of 16, the eldest daughter fell in love with a street hawker and eloped with him. This came as a shock to her mother because her daughter had been performing very well in school and had expressed the desire to become a schoolteacher. Moreover, she had taken the small amount of jewelry and some cash her mother had been collecting to marry her off. Not knowing where to turn, the mother approached Veeran for help. Veeran suggested they file a case against the boy of forcible abduction and rape since the girl was a minor. However, when they went to the police station to register an FIR, they learnt that the couple had already filed a report against the mother in which it was stated that the girl had run away with the boy of her own free will and that her mother was coercing her to return because she was planning to have her trafficked (*dhandha karana chaahti hai*). Veeran told me, "Even I was stumped at the audacity of the girl." The police had actually not registered a formal FIR and, but for Veeran's intervention, they might have seen this as an opportunity to extract money from both sides. In view of the gravity of the accusation levelled by the daughter, the police advised her mother to "settle" with the girl and her boyfriend. "Did you have to settle with the police too?" I had asked, for I would never have used terms like bribe, and her mother had said in a matter of fact way *"unka to bannta tha."* This expression is difficult to translate but it implies that it was money owed to the police, much as gifts are owed to affines.[9] Money was paid to the police, and the complaint filed by the girl and her partner was suppressed.[10] "Forget about the jewelry," the policeman told the girl's mother. "You are lucky to not have landed in jail under the new Domestic Violence Act." As happens in many such cases, the boy abandoned the girl once they had run out of the money obtained from selling the jewelry and she came back begging for forgiveness. She was then pregnant but Veeran was able to use her influence to coerce a boy who had previously been caught in petty thieving to marry the pregnant girl and so the matter was resolved for all intents and purposes. I once met the girl when she had come visiting her mother with a child in tow and, according to her mother, her daughter was happy and the boy's family would not dare to misbehave with her as they know she had Veeran as a guardian of sorts. With heavy irony, Veeran had once said to me "god sometimes chooses the worst of people to do the best of deeds – put that in the notebook you carry around and swallow these words." I did swallow these words, but some stories do not have happy endings.

We Want Just a Little Help

Newspapers on September 14, 2008, had carried headlines about serial bomb blasts in Delhi. As the *Economic Times* reported, "Terror hit busy marketplaces in Delhi on Saturday, claiming around 30 lives and injuring 90 in five bomb blasts across Karol Bagh, Connaught Place and Greater Kailash. The Indian Mujahideen, which security agencies have confirmed is just another nomenclature for Simi, has claimed responsibility for the blasts in an e-mail sent minutes before the serial blasts."

I might remind the reader that SIMI is the abbreviation for Students, Islamic Movement of India. First established in 1977 as a student movement in Aligarh, it has had a checkered legal history. It was first designated as a terrorist organization by a government notification in 2001 and banned. The ban was contested, lifted in 2008 by the Delhi High Court, and reinstated by the Supreme Court in the same year. Several of its members have been arrested at various times under the provisions of various anti-terror laws such as TADA, POTA, MCOCA and the Unlawful Activities (Prevention) Act, as I described in the last chapter. Here I confine myself to a single example of how such arrests and threats of prosecution affect relations within local communities. My point is to ask if the quotidian practices of policing I described get redefined in the context of concerns about national security and become lethal to sustaining the everyday life of communities.

Right in the wake of the 2008 bomb blasts, one of the young Muslim men in one of my field sites – a resettlement colony in East Delhi – who made a small income from teaching elementary Arabic in a small neighborhood madrasa, was arrested for being a member of SIMI. But before he was arrested, he had been asked to report to the local police station every day as he was under suspicion of having aided in the bomb blast by acting as a conduit for money for a collaborator from Pakistan. As it happened, there was not much evidence the police could get against him, and the local police were under a lot of pressure from "higher-ups" to produce some culprits from the Muslim areas so that they could show how actively they were pursuing the cases. The particular Muslim area the police inquiries zoomed in on was a resettlement colony, in which Muslim families displaced from old Delhi in the notorious beautification and sterilization drive during the National Emergency of 1976 were relocated (see Tarlo 2003). The police officers in charge of the investigations, with little knowledge of the area, might have easily thought that there must be continuing resentment against the government in these areas. The high rate of thefts, inter-clan rivalries, suspicion of Bengali-speaking Muslims as illegal immigrants, and even murders that had little to do with national security and much more to do with political rivalries at the neighborhood level, made this area "ripe for the picking" as Mahfooz, a local activist, informed me. Under pressure from the higher officials and having decided that the matter was beyond their limited jurisdiction, the policemen posted at the local level gave the names of several relatives and friends of this young man to the higher-level police. One of the relatives was the brother-in law and maternal cousin of the accused. The police then rounded up several of these relatives but began to pay special attention to this particular cousin.

It was a matter of open discussion among the family members of the accused that he was innocent and that the younger cousin was being pressured to say that he knew where material for making crude bombs had been hidden. If he were to sign a statement to this effect the police would then prepare a "spot report" to produce in court showing "recovery." I do not know whether the accused or his cousin were subjected to brutal beating or torture because I came to know of these events only after a period of several years and after the police had decided that this was not a strong enough case to take forward. However, the young cousin's mother told me that her son was not only threatened by the police officers that they would ensnare him in a false case if he did not give evidence against the accused, but that he was also subjected to beatings and obscenities. It was, she said, a case of one police officer beating up the accused to sign a confession and another beating up my son to sign a witness statement. Alternately after getting a beating, another policeman would offer the lure of money, a flat in a posh area, a government job, if my son cooperated with them in making up the false case. She did not know if her son would have been strong enough to endure this treatment for a long time but for some inscrutable reason, the police lost interest in this particular accused who was released with the warning that he should not get involved in politics and should stick to his everyday routines.

However, everyday routines were precisely what were threatened by the penetration of the new demands in what were settled practices in the transactions between local police and the higher-level police officers. The theme of how harm done to one person does not remain confined to him but percolates within the family, within wider kinship networks, and even within the community, is what Lotte Buch Segal (2018) characterizes as "tattered" kinship. I had not realized the extent to which the local knowledge of the low-level police officers can acquire lethal forms, thinking previously that it would be deployed at the local level for extracting bribes or distributing favors (see also de Sardan 1999). However, now it seems to me that what appear to be events on a different scale altogether cannot be completely separated from quasi events in the neighborhood. In the areas I am familiar with, it is not some general processes of modernity or of tradition that are leading to the erosion of communities, but the specific practices of policing and surveillance and these need close attention. We do have the help of some excellent works in the vernacular by survivors who have not only provided important testimonial literature but also written with great insight on these matters. In the next chapter I will take up these insights and pose the question of when and under what conditions do these life forms that I have delineated here become corroded, producing the inhuman from the ruins of the human?

A Time for Pause

In thinking of the dispersed body of the police, I have given some thought to the way different scales come to be enmeshed in each other so that measuring things through applying a standard measure to two different objects becomes different from, say, *taking a measure* of things, asking how does a feeling of rightness arise? In these provisional concluding thoughts, I would like to put forward some observations on context that need to be made explicit at this stage as markers for new questions. The strong influence of Peirce on semiotics has meant that anthropologists privilege the notations in the logical structure of signs provided by Peirce (1955) and hence the notion of context has been taken up primarily through the semiotic device of the index and context-dependent references in texts. But outside of texts, in concrete situations when we are standing face to face, we don't need to decipher who is the person behind the pronoun "you" because you are before me. In such situations, how might we want to think of expressions and actions as together standing in need of specification of context?

In his remarkable expansion of Wittgenstein's remarks on context, Cavell (1979) speaks of two different senses in which we might speak of context in relation to concepts in our everyday life. There is, first, the rather simple case of expressions for which we cannot find an appropriate context. We do not know in advance which context would be the right one – as Wittgenstein's famous example of the rose having no teeth shows (in contrast to the baby having no teeth), for if the rose did have teeth, where could we imagine these teeth to be located? The second case is that in which we already have some sense of where an expression belongs and thus also a sense of what might be the *right* context for it. Figuring out the route of projection of such an expression, determining where it belongs, then, becomes a matter of hitting on the right context that would give us a feeling of its rightness, not through the application of predetermined rules, but through the experiences we have with each other within a form of life. We might, indeed, find a new context for the use of a familiar expression, or a practice, but then we have to figure out if the new context provides us with an instance of this *old* concept or if we need another concept to figure out why that was wrong and this is right.

In the case of such concepts as bribery, gift, punishment, document, when applied to police procedures, people can decipher a rightness of context when they expect that going into the police station to register a

case will require that a local don, or a *jaankar* (knowledgeable person), or a woman such as Veeran, come
with them to provide the necessary mediation (Das
2014, 2020). But when the young man as the accused I
described, or his cousin, are taken to a police station and
a different landscape of police procedures opens up that
they have to decipher on the go – we might ask, might
we not, if this is another instance of the old concepts
of policing they had? Could they "naturally" extend or
project their understanding of bribery or punishment to
this new situation? How will they determine if the new
context in which they find themselves is to be taken as
an instance of the old concept? Or do they now have to
invent new concepts? Concepts, for Wittgenstein, are
the whole range of words, gestures, actions, through
which the normativity of the concept – its tolerance and
intolerance of new projections – is grown out of the
experience in *this* form of life and not in another (Das
2020). Does this shifting of contexts tell us something
new about legal fictions? This was the second question I
posed in the opening pages of this chapter and to which
I return now.

In classical common law jurisprudence, legal fictions
are either considered to be plain falsehoods that are
scandalous for the law or necessary inventions produced
by the law itself (Samuel 2015; Thomas et al. 2011).
Bentham famously stated that fictions were falsehoods
and that a judge who invents them should be sent to
jail. Even when it was acknowledged that a legal fiction
could have beneficial effects, it was considered too crude
an instrument to achieve such ends (see Polloczek 1999).
There were others for whom legal fictions derived their
vitality from people and could provide some guarantee that law could keep pace with changing situations.
Classic examples of legal fictions were that a contract
that was made at sea could be treated as a contract made

at the Royal Exchange since that was the necessary
condition for the contract to be valid. Mitchell (1893)
gives the example from Roman Law in which a father
had the right to sell his son into slavery and even if the
master freed the slave, the father could claim the same
rights of ownership over his son. Mitchell contends that
in order to aid the son to gain his freedom, the law was
modified so that if the son had been sold three times and
freed each time, then he was no longer the property of
the father. In many cases the act of the father selling the
son and the buyer freeing him was done almost synchro-
nously. Here are fictions, then, that were used to bring
the law in consonance with changing norms. At the
heart of the issue for Mitchell is that while the classical
definition of a legal fiction defined it as the law treating
the true as the false *but not impossible*; he (Mitchell)
offers a modification to the effect that legal fictions are
devices to conceal the fact that a judicial decision is not
fully in accord with the law – and hence that judges not
only interpret the law but they also make the law. He
attributes the vitality of law to this particular capacity
of distinction between legal fictions and lies.

Seen from this perspective, how should we see the
fiction of the dutiful police officer (false in this case but
not impossible) and the recovery from the house of the
abductor (possible and made true through the documents produced in court although we are in no position
to decide which of the stories circulating in the neighborhood was true)? We can, however, see that that the
judge is able to use both these "facts" to give a judgment
which seemed just, especially when one thinks of the
testimony of the body of the little girl whose grievous
wounds were there for all to see and who even as she
stammered, for part of her tongue had been sliced by
the abductor, could point decisively toward the abductor and say "that uncle" when asked who had inflicted

the injuries on her. That the police followed proper procedure and that the recovery narrative left no legal loopholes for the defense to exploit, was also a component of this narrative in court. As a minor girl who had been raped, the medical evidence alone would be sufficient for a judgment of statutory rape yet the question of fiction here does not stem from the jurist's concerns of whether it is allowing the judge to make law rather than interpret it; or the concern that law can keep pace with changing times: what was at stake was the concreteness of *this case, this girl, and this milieu* within which the law needed to provide her protection. I, for one, imagine the eight-year-old, standing bravely before the judge and, when asked if she could identify the person who had done such cruel acts to her, turns to the man on trial and pointing her finger at him says, "that uncle ji, he did this to me." Perhaps like the case of the naked soldier that Cora Diamond (2001) analyzes, who is an enemy but who, at a moment caught in his nakedness by the armed opponent who cannot bring himself to fire, seems simply a human being exposed in all his vulnerability, there is a fleeting recognition here too that the life of law is a human form of life. We cannot trust this to happen every time, but we should permit ourselves to hope that it can happen sometimes.

4
Detecting the Human: Under Which Skies Do We Theorize?

The preceding two chapters took an oblique look at the theme of inordinate knowledge as the stories of what transpired in prisons, police stations, or rooms in which accused were tortured, or abducted and trafficked children sequestered, seeped into the neighborhoods. Sometimes such knowledge took the form of rumors; at other times the knowledge of such events hid behind insinuations made during verbal duels; and, at still other times, it was carried by words that just broke loose from the immediate contexts of their utterances to carry the aura of some other reality. In a brief summary of the course content of Foucault's 1984 lectures, *The courage of truth* (2011), Frédéric Gros puts the lectures in the context of the time between Foucault's last illness and his death. In Gros's words: "It is difficult to know precisely what knowledge Foucault had and wanted to have of the illness that was weakening him" (p. 347). Noting that, though regularly treated at the Tarnier hospital in Paris, Foucault did not ask for or receive any diagnosis, Gros then goes on to say, "This is a question of the personal relationship each individual has with his or her body, illness, and death. It remains that some of the readings put forward in 1984 of great texts from the history of philosophy are situated precisely in this horizon of illness and death" (Gros 2011: 347). The final paragraph of Gros's summary states, "Foucault can thus write these words, which he will not have time to utter, but which are the last words he wrote on the last page of the manuscript of his final lecture: '*What I would like to stress in conclusion is this: there is no establishment of the truth without an essential position of otherness; the truth is never the same; there can be truth only in the form of the other world and the other life (l'autre mond et de la vie autre)*'" (p. 356, original emphasis).

In this last phrase, Gros gets a glimpse of the philosopher who becomes someone, who, through the courage of his truth-telling makes the "lightning flash of an otherness flash through his life and speech" (p. 356). What I have to offer in this book is at some level something very different but it still relates to knowing something about truths and fictions. My truth tellers don't make any claims to philosophy; they are minor figures until, like Wahid Shaikh, propelled into national attention by happenstance, and yet it is in their lives that I am trying to find the stars to which my own writing fate (a wagon of sorts) is hitched.[1] Wahid Shaikh courageously lived through six years of torture and imprisonment but he converts every experience into moments of self-learning in his writing – what did I do *wrong* when I kept silent in court when asked in the formulaic questions of the judge, whether anyone had mistreated me, or pressurized me, or if I had any complaints, he asks? And he learns that his mistake was to have let himself get so frightened that not only did he not utter a word in court except to say "no" to the questions on physical harm or intimidation put to him by the judge; he even let the police intimidate him into asking his brother to withdraw a complaint he had prepared with the help of a local Muslim leader. Instead, what should he have done, in this kind of scene of intimidation and terror?

As an example of the courage of truth, here are two recommendations on how to conduct yourself when you fall into the clutches of the police from Wahid Shaikh's (2017) book, in my free translation.

> If the police have ensnared you in a false case, then forget the fact that you know how to sign your name. *Break your thumb*, but do not put your signature on any paper under any conditions. Even if the police say, these are your bail papers or these are your discharge papers, *even then* do not sign them. These are forgeries. ... There is only one way to save yourself from the false recoveries (of weapons or ammunition) they will ask you to confess to – let yourself die but do not sign any paper. (p. 117)

> During the narco-test, you should remain absolutely silent. Do not answer any question posed by the doctor ... if they are harassing you by asking the same questions repeatedly then start reciting *kalima-ai-tayyiba* and *durood sharif* at the top of your voice[2] ... never repeat what they have said. For example, the doctor will say, repeat after me, "I did not take part in the bomb blast." Just say, "I am innocent" ... similarly do not repeat any sentence which has a negative clause. For example, do not say, "I did not go to Pakistan." They will alter the negative statement into an affirmative one. (p. 385)

In contrast to Wahid's courage in making this story of torture and forced confessions public through his writing, Kh's story comes into the public domain in a different way. People in the neighborhood know what happened to her, but they do not dwell on her story which has over the years merged with other stories of the disappearance of children, or rumors about some girl who was spotted in one of the brothels at G. B. Road with whispered conversations about whether the girl was abducted or sold into prostitution. The Institute for Socio-Economic Research on Development and Democracy (ISERDD), through a tuition support scheme, has supported Kh's mother with some small monetary contributions to help pay for private tuition Kh needs in order to cope with school work (she was in seventh grade last year); sometimes she likes to share stories she writes with the ISERDD staff with whom I work closely.[3] One of them is a story about a little girl's escape from the death-room (*kaal kothri*) her evil (*bhayanak*)[4] uncle, who is really a *rakshasa* (demon), has put her in. In this story a girl, similar to Kh, is abducted and even though brutally injured, she manages to escape one day when the evil uncle is out plying his three-wheeler, and his wife has stepped out in the street to buy something from a hawker. Left for that moment with the two children who are instructed by their mother to shout out to her if the girl steps out from the room, she lures them into playing hide and seek. As they count to one hundred maintaining a slow rhythm – one – two – three – four – with their eyes closed and covered with their hands, she runs out and, taking the meandering narrow lanes, so narrow that no vehicle can possibly be driven on them, and avoiding the main road, she reaches the main market where a crowd immediately gathers around her seeing as she was so badly injured and looked as if she was being pursued by some monster. By now her abductor, who does not actually look like a *rakshasa* at all, has come on his three-wheeler to the same market looking for her. He tries to tell the crowd that she is his niece and is mentally deranged. But the little girl clings to a kind-looking man and will not let go of his hand as she clutches at his shirt, trembling. "Don't let him take me, *bhaiya*," she sobs uncontrollably, "he is the one who has done all this to me." The crowd, now fueled by anger (*aag baboola ho kar*) turns as one on the man and drags him to the nearby police station manned by constables other than the one who was investigating her case and so she is rescued and returned to her parents and the evil uncle, who had done "bad, bad, things" to her is put in prison.

A great story, I tell her, your Hindi writing is really improving. I do not ask her if this is an account of a true story, or an account of a nightmare, or perhaps an episode from a TV show, because whenever I see her I let her take the lead in what she wants to speak about. Questions make her very uneasy.

Shaikh's book and Kh's story are truths of a different nature (albeit deeply contested ones), than the ones that Foucault discusses from classical Greek philosophy, though it is important to preserve the fragile connections between truth and fiction. How is one to consider the character of the kind of knowledge which is also somewhere on the horizon, not between one's own illness and death, but between cruelty and death in these milieus? Let us consider what kind of otherness is brought into plain view when we contemplate such questions as how we live with the knowledge that torture is routinely practiced in our society as Wahid tells us; or that every riot and mass killing in pogroms that punctuate political life in India has the ability to wound one who contemplates it; or that large numbers of children in India run away from home or are abducted or trafficked (Steinberg 2019) leading to the question – are these happenings the intimations of another reality that is not tucked away somewhere afar but is in a relation of nextness to the world we inhabit? Is it possible to contemplate the lower and upper limits of the human not as a metaphysical question but one that surfaces when we ask if the inhuman does not lie in monstrosities produced by nature or by any evil inherent in men and women, but is an eventuality of the human embedded within a form of life? In the acclaimed book, *Claim of reason*, Cavell (1979) provocatively states that "I would have been glad to have suggested that a correct relation between inner and outer, between a soul and its society is the theme of Investigations as whole." Cavell says that for anyone to claim a particular society as one's own, as I have argued elsewhere (Das 2020), entails a readiness to find ways of correcting what in this society might offend the soul. Remarkably, Cavell does not think of Wittgenstein as having said that the correct relation is to be found in a *society's* ability to correct the soul – but the soul's journey in correcting "its" society – of being able to define a correct relation between the inner and the outer. This understanding of the human complicates the question of the inhuman because it is not relying on such abstractions as that evil is inherent in human nature; or that the reason why one cannot exercise a judgment over the kinds of cruelties often perpetrated by minor actors implicated in torture or in mass killings is because such people were part of a machine and had no choice in the matter. Even if this formulation carries some weight, it is surely the beginning of a discussion but not its end.

Extreme Violence

One of the ways in which the question of the human surfaces in the literature in both social sciences and humanities is through the experience of extreme violence. It is striking that in the contemplation of extreme violence, whether in context of classroom discussions with students or in books on moral philosophy, in which the question of responsibility for genocides or mass rapes in war are discussed as hard cases, one often finds the query, how could ordinary human beings have committed such unspeakable atrocities? Sometimes with even greater sense of immediacy one asks, how could one's neighbors have become one's killers? (Das 2007, 2008; Kalyvas 2006).

In his famous prize-winning novel on the Rwandan genocide, *Murambi: The book of bones*, Boubacar Boris Diop (2006) adds an "Afterword" in which he tries to explain how a group of African writers assembled in Kilagi in 1998 to accomplish a collective project of placing themselves in the city and listening to the experiences of people during the massacres and later converting these accounts into individually authored literary productions. Their project was initially met with suspicion in Kilagi, especially as people learnt that it was funded by a French organization. The reader realizes that though these writers came to Rwanda filled with the right sentiments and were deeply moved by the vision of African solidarity, the team seems to have been woefully unprepared for this task. There they were, ready to listen to the victims of the massacre, their African brothers and sisters, to make their suffering known to the entire world through their books, yet one is stunned to hear Diop say,

> I did not know that in June 1994 the soldiers of the French military Operation Turquoise had for weeks on end and with full knowledge of the facts, played volleyball over the mass graves of Murambi, a fact that a billboard, still very much visible over the site, recalls. In short, I did not yet know that France had been, . . . 'at the heart of the genocide of the Tutsis'.

I cite this from Diop not to chastise him or anyone else for their naivety. As every researcher who has been present in one way or another on such scenes of mass violence knows, there is no way to avoid the discovery of one's own ignorance; that one stumbles upon facts of this nature sooner or later. I recall that working on the massacre of Sikhs in 1984 in Sultanpuri – a resettlement colony on the periphery of Delhi, which was one of the two sites of brutal massacres after the assassination of Mrs. Gandhi (see Das 2007) – we were befriended by a tearful man who looked quite devastated and who insisted on taking us around, but who later turned out to be one of the persons on the side of the killers during the riots. If our small team of researchers had not stuck around for the next two years, visiting the area on a daily basis, we would never have been able to decipher who to trust, or how to reconstruct the events that had happened, even though we were on the scene within two days of the killings. And thus it is that one applauds the efforts of human rights workers, literary figures, film makers, all of whom want to tell the story of extreme violence to the world. Those who are charged with these tasks follow the methods this team assembled in Rwanda followed, which was to travel all over Rwanda, follow stories they heard, and in that process, meet the characters of their future novels. "They often confessed to us that they understood nothing about what had happened to them, so that we sometimes suspected that they were, paradoxically, relying on us to penetrate the mystery of such a radical and consuming hatred" (Diop 2006: 184).

Indeed, as I have recounted in my recent book, *Textures of the ordinary* (Das 2020), it is a mystery that people are often inclined to trust a story to a stranger, rather than to someone intimate. Of course, there are also stories generated through court trials, or testimonies before "Truth and Reconciliation Commissions" (see Rojas-Perez 2017; Ross 2003; among others). However, as Richard Rechtman (2020, 2021) has perceptively observed, the testimonies and stories that surface from many of these situations are inevitably molded by the pressures of particular genres, and often these are stories of leaders or other powerful actors (in that sense the task of this team of writers was different from putting big actors on trial); they are not the stories of ordinary people who were also part of the killing machines. First, the very context of the storytelling gives these stories a certain coherence as when they are pressed to clarify what came before and what came after; or when the accounts are measured against a picture of what is an actual possibility; or conversely when the story is cast to show something monstrous or horrific in the character of the person before a tribunal or a court. Second, even the best of writers such as Primo Levi, when writing about their experiences, are pressured to make what happened in the Nazi camps legible or intelligible to those who have never experienced such horror and terror. For this task they have to keep the narrative within the bounds of sense.[5] Third, the very effort to fix culpability often leads to lengthy trials of those in positions of leadership so we do not hear about the ordinary life of ordinary executioners very often. None of these points make the archives of the trials in courts or literary renderings suspect, for such indeed are the conditions under which the very act of telling something even becomes possible. It does mean, however, that we need to see how our own research questions might become skewed in the directions in which the dominant stories lead us. Rechtman (2020) makes us face the fact that most testimony given by the major figures who exercised leadership in organizing the machines of massacre, regardless of the forms that genocide took, mostly evoked ideological grounds for justifying the massacres – the killings were political, I did not personally kill anyone, I did not personally benefit from the killing, these were the demands of the day for a new society to rise, and so on. Rechtman argues that the case of Rwanda was perhaps exceptional in that the principal actors who were identified as leaders were judged before an international tribunal, but the trials of a large number of ordinary participants took place in local tribunals and, as Rechtman (2020) notes, these local-level processes allowed one to get some under-standing of the everyday lives of small executioners. There are excellent studies now that track the difficul-ties of legal trials for such large numbers of accused as well as the pressures to resume a normality in Rwanda that put reconciliation in the name of national duty at the heart of the process.[6] I will not review this literature or visit the controversies it has generated here because I want to make only one point. Rechtman argues that our knowledge about conditions of genocide in dif-ferent formations – whether in Nazi camps or in the killing fields of Cambodia – often comes from the liter-ary works, from testimonies that seek to make future memory, or from court testimonies of major actors. I emphasize again that, however profound the literary works and the testimonies, and however systematic the interrogations in courts of law or in Commissions of Inquiry, the narrative structure within which stories are told puts the pressure on making what transpired in these spaces intelligible to those who cannot imag-ine what went on in these spaces. Thus, when Diop describes the expectations of those who told their sto-ries as their "relying on us to penetrate the mystery of such a radical and consuming hatred," I feel that he has already given a name (radical hatred) and a coherence to the overwhelming fact that *they could not understand* what had made neighbors turn into lethal killers. The people Diop and his colleagues talked to did not bring these experiences under the umbrella of an overarch-ing concept like radical hatred. Is it possible, then, that when we are faced with such inordinate knowledge, we might forgo the desire to assign names to the emotions or motives of actors, whether perpetrators or victims? Instead, we might follow closely the confusions that mark what I have elsewhere called a descent into the ordinary (Das 2007).

Rechtman manages to do just that on the basis of the archives of the Cambodian genocide and his own work in the psychiatry wards with survivors as well as ordinary perpetrators. The very title of his book, *La vie ordinaire des génocidaires*, shows that there is an ordinary life of ordinary killers who are incorporated in the killing machines as cogs with specific responsibilities they have to perform within a strict hierarchy of surveillance and punishment. Without their participation day in and day out in meeting targets, keeping the instruments of murder in order, removing the dead bodies, preparing the ground for new people to be brought in and executed, the scale of the genocide would have been impossible to achieve. We shall return to this point again but for now I simply ask: would the right move be to shift our questions, to not give them sharp edges?[7]

Shifting the Question

Hannah Arendt's phrase "the banality of evil" has almost become a default phrase in connection with any discussion of genocide or mass violence. Famously evoked in connection with the Eichmann trial, the phrase was simply indicating that Eichmann was an average, ordinary person (Arendt 1963). Rechtman rightly points out that what Arendt is asserting is not a metaphysical truth about good and evil, but rather she is creating a rationale for the claim that it was right that for all the horrific projects of the fascist state that he was responsible for, it is human justice he should face, it is a human court of law in which he is tried. Put simply, the phrase "the banality of evil" is indicating that Eichmann was ordinary, commonplace – neither a demon nor a monster. As an ordinary, commonplace man, it was only right that he should have been subjected to human justice. If one were to conceptualize Eichmann's participation in the killing machines of the Nazis as the work of the devil or of some other species of supernatural force, then one might have said that only divine justice will be able to accord him a punishment that is commensurate with the horrors he has perpetrated. But if he was just an ordinary man, made powerful by the very machinery of death he presided over, then what else but human justice with all its inadequacy, its disappointments, would be the appropriate conceptual and material space within which his crimes would be proclaimed and human punishment accorded. Divine justice will take its own course or not; it is not in our hands.

Where does the idea of evil come from in Arendt's argument and what purchase does it have when paired with banality? In response to this question Rechtman opens an important route for further travel. He argues that Arendt's interest in Eichmann comes from her long-standing interest in totalitarianism. The monstrosity lies here not in the person but in the incommensurability that the "evil" of totalitarianism, its stupendous violence, is enabled and served by the hands of completely mediocre men. After all, it is not because Eichmann is ordinary that he becomes susceptible to the totalitarian fascist killing machines. Rather, we should place the evil in the phrase "banality of evil" in the capability of totalitarian regimes to generate the killing apparatus, and as we shall see in the Conclusion, in the capabilities of Western democracies that took a lead in developing techniques of clean torture that leave no visible wounds on the body. It is because the totalitarian regimes of the Nazis or the Pol Pot regime were able to extract the labor of thousands and thousands of men (and women) to run the system – think of the small-time executioners, the ones who had to survey the fields, remove the dead bodies, clean up the mess to get the places readied for the next executions, whether in the gas chambers or the killing fields, *that the genocides happened*. Without their labor, no Eichmann or Duch, however evil, could have engineered the mass killings. Again and again, we will come back to the issue that Rechtman is insisting upon – what is in need of explanation is not how an ordinary person such as Eichmann or Duch could commit such evil, but how do we explain the fact that so many small executioners went about their daily lives in a way that killing for them just became routine.

The fascination in the literature with the extraordinary acts of cruelty itself stands in need of explanation. In the case of the Cambodian genocide, for instance, Hinton (1998) writes about the cultural resonance that the rare events of extracting the liver of the victims by Khmer Rouge and eating it carried in the rumors and even the talk among the executioners. Yet these were rare events in comparison to what the executioners and the victims were faced with in their everyday life.[8] In the case of riots and pogroms in India, every event creates some stories of the cruelty with regard to ripping open the stomach of a pregnant woman and flinging the fetus against a wall. Yet, as we saw in the cases of torture documented by Wahid Shaikh, there was an uncanny proximity of the physical torture and the constant flow of ordinary talk by ordinary police inspectors. Even in the case of torture inflicted on Kh, it was embedded in the routine acts of cooking and entrusting Kh with the task of looking after the two children of the abductor who resided in the same room. These are juxtapositions that are hard to understand and, frankly speaking, I am much more in sympathy with the question of how people like Wahid and Kh find routes back to the ordinary than in the question of testing if, given those conditions in which ordinary people became killers, I too would have become a killer. Perhaps I am just demonstrating the limits of my own moral life.

I am also intrigued by the fact that while the scale of killing in genocides might be attributed to the machinery of totalitarian regimes – what are we to make of the fact that democracies have devised their own machineries to tolerate the fact that torture routinely occurs within the legal apparatus itself. At least some moral projects are honed within the difficult circumstances of the everyday life of slums and poor neighborhoods of the kind that I have described in my work, but why are we less haunted by the apparatus of a democracy that carries on systematic torture than the apparatus of the totalitarian state?

A Form of Life

In a compelling paper on the social and the vital dimensions of forms of life, the philosopher Piergiorgio Donatelli (2019) asks us to recognize how the minute texture of the vital embodies both the sublime and the enervating, and how a whole form of life – splendid or miserable alike – is to be found in such minute moments. Against the inclination to take such minute conditionedness of life as a way of compromising the human, of losing track of it, Donatelli asks us to pay attention to the expected and unexpected continuations of ways of living, regardless of how great or miserable these ways of living appear to us. Instead of thinking of the critical as standing outside such moments of immersion, he finds a critical voice within such moments of the mutual absorption of the vital and the social. The minute nuances, he says, reveal an entire landscape, a whole way of living. What are these ways of living in which the human is not secured once and for all but must be secured within a form of life, repeatedly, diurnally? In this last concluding section, I turn to some ethnographic moments to show what is entailed in living a life in which one can simply ask: can I go on?

Obviously, what happens in the slums – the tempos and rhythms through which some aspects in the flow of life are given expression, others are wrapped in evasions, or the play between the definite and the indefinite – is quite different from the violence of the killing machines. But is there an absolute impermeable boundary between the extreme violence of genocides and the slow unfolding of moments that are fraught with incalculable risks of escalating or morphing into extreme violence? Stanley Cavell (2007b: xiii) comments on this issue in the context of his Foreword to my book *Life and words*:

> I was prompted to ask myself whether her cases of extreme manifestation of a society's internal, one could say, intimate and absolute violence are comprehensible as extreme states, or suddenly invited enactments, or a pervasive fact of the social fabric that may hide itself, or one might also say, may express itself, in everyday encounters. The background of my question is double, one part coming from a further perception of Das's, and one part coming from my having in recent years begun to register unacknowledged yet inevitable manifestations of what Wittgenstein pictures as the pervasive, irreducible recurrence of human nervousness or restlessness, as it were the human incapacity for and refusal of peace . . . a kind of perpetual preparation for violence that has led me to speak of our dealings among ourselves "the little deaths of everyday life," the slights, the grudges, the clumsiness, the impatience, the bitterness, the narcissism, the boredom and so on (variously fed and magnified and inflamed by standing sources of social enmity, say, racism, sexism, elitism, and so on).

What is crucial here is to consider the swirling affects, the hurly-burly of life in which not only are multiple durations intersecting in crazy curves but there is also a close embrace of what is laughter and what is grief; what is safety and what is danger; how might one allude to something yet not say it and the constant possibility of lethal transfigurations. Your daughter may turn out to have the vocabulary of a slut; you might find that you have to tread carefully to avoid getting into disputes but you end up in court or prison; or an ordinary act of taking part in a demonstration might mark you as a future suspect in terror-related cases. I want to try to think how this is a particular register of inordinate knowledge – excessive knowledge that spills out and propels life in directions over which one loses control completely. This is not purely a matter of general conditions of uncertainty but an essential feature of the kinds of dangers that are simply folded into the crossings people have to make every day, the thresholds that become thickened with how such inordinate knowledge has had to be absorbed in the thick of everyday life.

I invite the reader into three ethnographic scenes, to convey the color of experiences that have helped me to shift the gaze away from retrospective accounts that project a deep history into their descriptions of contingent moments of everyday life as if the eventual is already standing at the doorstep of the actual. Instead, I want to find the language to convey the contingency of unfolding events, deeply familiar and at the same time deeply strange.

The First Scene

The first scene I describe is drawn from a small network of friends from a neighborhood that has seen sectarian riots, minor altercations, frequent instances of crimes such as murder and intimidation, and, for young men, the threat of addiction. The eight young men described here are in their mid-twenties, all of them unmarried and with varying degrees of instability in their jobs. Four of them are Hindu and four are Muslim. They have been friends since their first grade as all of them went to the same neighborhood school. One of these men was part of a writing project that I had instituted with two small groups (five persons in each group) of first-generation college students (from my study areas) registered in the non-collegiate program for an undergraduate degree at Delhi University. The idea was for each group to write short accounts of their experiences on any one issue and share it among themselves and with members of ISRDD for purposes of discussion of larger issues. We were able to run these discussion groups for a couple of years with intermittent meetings, but they were hard to sustain as participants found part-time jobs or lost interest. Nevertheless, here is an excerpt from Sonu, resident of a low-income neighborhood from West Delhi.

Writing Excerpt from June 2018 (translated from Hindi)
A custom (English word used in the original) that has grown among my circle of friends[9] is that twice a month we go to see a movie together and then we eat outside.[10] Each person in this circle of friends bears the expenditure in turn and chooses which film we will see and where we will eat. This time it was Farooq's turn and he was insistent that he wanted to see *"Padmaavat."* We argued and we cajoled and we tried everything to dissuade him from going to this particular film but he was not in a mood to listen. What can one do, we thought now – we will have to go but we are very apprehensive because anything could happen.

Sony had copied the following news item culled from a Hindi newspaper after this opening statement.

नई दिल्ली। संजय लीला भंसाली की फिल्म पद्मावत को लेकर चल रहा विवाद थमने का नाम नहीं ले रहा है। फिल्म पद्मावत के खिलाफ अपना प्रदर्शन जारी रखते हुए श्री राजपूती करणी सेना ने शुक्रवार को सेंसर बोर्ड

के अध्यक्ष प्रसुन जोशी को जयपुर साहित्य उत्सव के दौरान जयपुर नहीं आने की धमकी दी है। सेना ने धमकी दी है कि अगर वह जयपुर आए तो बुरी तरह पीटे जाएंगे। करणी सेना के अध्यक्ष सुखदेव सिंह गोगामेदी ने एक वीडियो संदेश के माध्यम से कहा कि फिल्म को रिलीज़ करने वालों और फिल्म के समर्थन में कुछ भी बोलने वालों को जयपुर में प्रवेश नहीं करने दिया जाएगा। उन्होंने कहा कि फिल्म का नाम पद्मावती से पद्मावत करने से वे लोग संतुष्ट नहीं है। वे फिल्म पर पूर्ण प्रतिबंध चाहते हैं।

Roughly translated, the news item reads as follows:

The ongoing controversy on Sanjay Leela Bhansali's film *Padmaavat* shows no sign of abatement. Continuing their agitation against the film the President of the Karni Sena issued a threat against Prasoon Joshi, the Head of the Censor Board on Friday, that he should refrain from coming to Jaipur during the Jaipur literary festival. The Sena has threatened that if he comes to Jaipur, he will be beaten up. The head of Karni Sena, Sukhdev Singh Gogamodi, has said through video messaging that those who have allowed the film to be released and those who plan to say anything in favor of the film will not be allowed to enter Jaipur. He said that changing the name of the film to *Padmaavat* (from the original *Padmavati*) has not satisfied them. They want the film to be prohibited.

A Coda on Padmaavat

This news item and others that Sonu has copied or referred to in his writing pertained to a controversy that had surrounded the production and release of this movie in 2018. It was part of the controversies that groups like the Karni Sena, with overt or covert support from the Bharatiya Janata Party (BJP), had courted over Rajput honor that started with the protests they waged over the banning of the glorification of the custom of sati by a legislative act (Prevention of Sati Act, 1987). Several Rajput groups then took to street-level protests and filed challenges in court over the right to celebrate their "customs." Periodic controversies over other films such as *Jodha Akbar*, which contained the theme of Rajput women being given in marriage to Muslim kings, had been waged earlier. The director and producer of *Padmaavat*, however, had emphasized that the film portrayed a fictional account based on an epic poem written by the Sufi mystic poet Mallik Mohammad Jayasi in 1540 on the Muslim Sultan Allaudin Khilji's desire for the princess Padmini of Chittor. It was not a film about any historical event. Earlier films in Hindi and Tamil based on this legend had not raised any controversies.[11] Clearly *Padmaavat* was not the kind of provocative hate literature written in late nineteenth, early twentieth century such as *Rangeela Rusul* (*The Colorful Prophet*) around which riots and colonial flare-ups happened (see, especially, Mehta 2012). So, one interesting question is why had the film raised so much controversy in 2018? What was once seen as a celebration and glorification of Rajput valor had now been recast as an insult to Hindu sensibilities.[12]

Most commentators on the controversy around the film have attributed it to the intensification of communalism with the rise of the nationalist rhetoric that not only perpetuates suspicion against Muslims but also tolerates random acts of violence such as public lynching of Muslims.[13] What is of interest to me is the kind of atmosphere of distrust such events and their reporting in the media have created at the local level. The issue that confronted Sonu, as it does many others, is how to sustain ordinary relations of work, or of friendship, or neighborly exchanges across the Hindu–Muslim divide?

Maintaining Friendships in Difficult Times

Just two or three days after Sonu's journal entry, I was in a discussion group of eight young men and women and the topic that emerged from the different concerns expressed by this group was whether Islam, "the religion of Muslims," was *kattar* – inflexible, intolerant. Two of the participants argued passionately that Hindus were "by nature" gentle, even cowardly, while Muslims could do "anything" in the name of their religion. I asked how many of those present had any Muslim friends (by happenstance all the participants that day were Hindus); four of them belonged to the lower caste categories such as Jatav, two were from middle-level castes labeled as Other Backward Castes, while two belonged to upper rungs of the caste hierarchy. It turned out that no one was willing to claim any Muslim as a "friend" with the exception of Sonu, who came from a small sub-caste of Brahmins. However, all had occasion to recall some interactions with Muslims during work, or during elections, or in the case of two of the participants, there was the give and take of ordinary neighborhood relations such as helping children with homework, or watching TV shows together. Some participants opined that earlier prohibitions on sharing of food had loosened among different castes and this had also influenced the everyday texture of relations with Muslims. Three participants offered examples of how considerate their Muslim acquaintances had been, when occasions for hospitality arose, respecting their sensitivities as Hindus who had to observe dietary restrictions as part of their religiosity. For example, one of the participants recalled that a Muslim neighbor would invite her to have tea but make it a point to get the milk from outside so that there was no suspicion that the milk might have been kept in a vessel next to one in which meat was cooked. In the same breath, there were other accounts of "cheating" – both Hindu and Muslim workers cheated at work, everyone agreed, but the scale of Muslim cheating was much higher. The form of talk was premised with qualifiers, "I do not say that Muslims don't belong here," followed by "they eat the food of this country (*ann yahan ka khate hain*), they should learn to be loyal to this country." (The use of negation in this locutionary form precisely affirms what is being denied.) But the ultimate test of the Muslim being *kattar*, most participants said, was that unlike Hindus who go to the *mazars* of the *pirs* (Muslim saints), no Muslim would ever go to a Hindu temple. "Would Muslims even be allowed into Hindu temples?" I asked. No one was very clear as to what would happen if a Muslim were to turn up at a Hindu temple but they were all sure of one thing – even if temple entry was allowed to Muslims, they would not go because their religion prohibits them showing respect to anyone except their Allah or their prophet, or even respect to their own saints, one of the participants said. "We are all *kafirs* for them," said another. There was, of course, some truth in their stories, though the matter was much more complicated. I refrained from giving any parallels with, say, the Hindu usage of the derogatory term *mlecha*, or the more colloquial *musalla* to designate Muslims because of the endless tangles that resort to parallelism might have created. Instead, I asked, "Why does it matter to *you* if a Muslim does not go to a temple?"

At this point, Sonu who had been listening quietly, said "yes, indeed, why should it matter? There are so many irresolvable things in our lives, why should I not enjoy what we have together rather than torture myself speculating if my friends would or would not go to a temple if Muslims were allowed in temples?" Now, others jumped into the fray and demanded, "Do you ever discuss these matters with your friends?" Sonu replied, "No, we don't discuss these things." "Why not?" A bit exasperated Sonu said, "If you wanted to preserve a plant, would you give it water, or would you

give it poison? Aren't there other things to talk about?"
"Still, you say that all through your childhood you
studied with them and you people have been friends
for a long, long, time. Surely you would have this much
understanding of each other that you can discuss things
frankly with each other?"

Turning to me, Sonu said,

> Aunty the thing is this. In our locality, there are small skir-
> mishes that arise over anything – who has thrown garbage
> in front of my house? Which boy passed a comment on
> my sister when she was passing by on the way to school?
> Who was the visitor in that house who was secretly taking
> pictures of the street? Who was seen exchanging a packet
> for money – is he a new drug peddler? My friends and I
> avoid discussing anything that might blow up and create
> a *hungama* (a tumultuous disturbance) – *koi hangama na
> khada ho jaaye.*

One of the participants said, "See you cannot really
trust your Muslim friends – otherwise why do you think
a disturbance would be created?" Sonu went on to say,
repeatedly and forcefully, that one had to choose one's
words carefully, but sometimes, he said, he felt defeated
by the onslaught of the kind of talk others were engaging in. Then, he felt he might end up saying anything,
anap-shanap, meaningless nonsense. Gradually he too
got dragged into the discussion within the terms others
had set for him and started giving counter-examples.
"The Muslim porters who take you up to Vaishno Devi,
the sacred shrine of the ten-armed Hindu goddess, shout
'*Jai Mata Di* – Hail to the Mother' – throughout the
journey; during the months of the closure of temples
in the higher reaches of the Himalayas when all priests
move to lower ground, it is Muslim caretakers who see
that the heavier idols that cannot be moved are kept
fed and worshipped." In this cascade of examples and

counter-examples, Sonu's original point about care for others taking the form of care for the words you use or refrain from using, his point about friendship being like the plant you keep alive by giving it water and not poison, was lost.

Sonu had completed his journal entry with the following words, "We persuaded Farooq to avoid going on the day the film would be released; we promised we would find another day to go." It seemed that they finally settled for a night of watching another movie in Sonu's house, a pirated video and dinner at their favorite *dhaba*. Sonu wrote, "I feel exasperated that Farooq just did not want to understand why we were so scared – suppose some Karni Sena fellows or some other outfit of the RSS type, were to come to disrupt the movie they would surely latch on to this Muslim-looking guy and it is not as if the police would come in time." Sonu and I both understood what "in time" meant here. As it turned out these fears were not unwarranted. After the Supreme Court had refused to entertain any petition banning the film, the release date was set for January 25, 2018, but many of the multiplex halls cancelled the screening of the film for fear of violence; a school bus was attacked by protestors; and in a small hall in another town two young men were arrested for hurling a petrol bomb at a cinema hall where the film was being screened.

I regard the scene of fear and apprehension of being attacked by members of the Karni Sena I have presented here as a "real possibility" as distinct from a "logical possibility."[14] The circle of friends tried to decipher the dangers of being identified as "Muslim" for one of them who bore all the identifying marks of being a Muslim in the tense scenario of the film being shown in the middle of an extremely tense situation. At the same time, they recognized that all kinds of desires might erupt – desires that could have been just ordinary desires for a film, for

an evening out, nothing that required so much discussion but that would have been simply taken for granted
in some other milieu, but not in this one. Farooq's
insistence – *dekhni hai to dekhni hai* – want to see it,
have to see it – is a form of desire they are all familiar
with. Another Muslim friend within the circle had said
to Sonu "sometimes one wants to just do an ordinary
thing – like see a film and not worry about whether you
look Muslim or you look Hindu – we will eventually
see the film but not in the way we wanted." I imagine
that words, and laughter, and song, probably filled up
the room where Sonu's parents had arranged for them
to see a video over tea and snacks. Recalling an earlier
episode, Sonu had told me, "Once my friend's parents
had to go to the village because they got embroiled in
a land dispute and for three years Farooq stayed in my
house. At first it was supposed to be for a few days, then
months, then years – but my mummy did not grudge
it. She loves Farooq like he was my brother." Through
an earlier entry about parents and their anxieties about
children growing up, I had learnt that Sonu's "mummy
ji" had lost one child to addiction and was terrified that
Sonu might fall into bad company like his brother had.
She cherished his friends because whatever they did,
they did it openly. These observations came up when
we were once discussing another film, *Uddada Punjab*,
which was on the theme of drug addiction. I learnt a lot
on how to engage the issues that were pressing for these
young people through the writing projects, especially
that caring for your words can take many forms.

There are many complex strands in this story that I
cannot fully unravel here. But I suggest that attention to
the possible is braided in this story within a milieu that
bears not only diffused memories of past riots, individual fights, or strains that become visible when, say, a girl
from one community elopes with a man from another

one, but also signs of the intensification of Hindu militancy against Muslims in recent years. Yet, the upsurge of desires also defies the milieu. Such desires, sometimes quotidian, sometimes transgressive, are recognized even though not always voiced among the circle of friends. They do not dismiss these desires entirely but they do try to contain them. The most interesting observation Sonu made is in the register of an ordinary realism (see Laugier 2015, 2018; Motta 2019) that does not want to put too much strain on the friendship across sectarian divisions. In order to maintain that friendship, language has to be carefully guarded. In this conception of realism, language is internal to reality rather than being seen as representing one or other aspect of reality that is independent of language and is to be found facing you front-on. This view of the real is not premised on a strict correspondence theory since the contingency inherent in the notion of the possible makes the fit between the conceived dangers and aspects of the real a less than perfect fit. Yet Sonu's conception of what language is doing in their lives poses a serious challenge to the trickery behind thought experiments that end up challenging the real by what Austin (1946) demonstrated to be a kind of metaphysical wile in which one is asked how one might prove something to be real, say about an object (such as bread), which one has never had any occasion to doubt as being real, in the first place. Instead, the anchoring of the possible to the real here recognizes the deeply contextual nature of the real which might take away the solidity of a reality that is simply out there but reinstates a reality that is being constantly made through the care or lack of it with which one wields words.

The Second Scene

In the case of *Begunah Qaidi* (*The innocent prisoner*), it was the way Wahid turned the encounter with enormous pain and insults into pedagogical moments for those who are likely to be imprisoned and tortured in the *future*, that was awesome but also showed how a human impulse to master this experience within this form of life (or death) showed up at the most horrifying moments. To give just two examples:

> The accused in the 7/11 case have submitted a detailed written account of the torture that was inflicted before police custody, after that, and what was inflicted in the prison in the MCOCA courts ... we have gathered together information on all the forms of torture inflicted on them ... and in the light of the judgments by higher courts and experiences we have also written out some advice so that the reader can imprint the suggestions on their hearts and minds. (Shaikh 2017: 36)

As part of this advice, consider these two important exhortations. First, Shaikh informs the reader (imagined mostly as a Muslim youth who is likely to fall into the net of the police) that stripping the prisoner naked is the standard operating procedure for the police. Every accused is stripped (lit. "made") naked before and after torture. In this state, he tells you, police will indulge in obscene actions and vulgar talk with you. You will be displayed in this state, to your relatives, your brother, your sister, your wife, your children, your parents, your friends. You will think why do I put up with this dishonor? It is better for me to sign whatever confession or paper they want me to sign. And then, as one might recall, Shaikh says with the absolute authority of having lived with this experience and having mastered it:

Remember, you have not become naked out of your own will. You have not become naked to commit any dirty or obscene act. You have been *made* naked for the only reason that you must agree to the false story being crafted by the police. For the duration in which the police keeps you without clothes (*belibas*) do not curse yourself. . . . Bear with it. For this Allah will give you good returns because you are bearing all this for the sake of truth. (Shaikh 2017: 370)

We do not have much theorization of how the naked body became such a potent symbol of dishonor not only in torture chambers but also in the language deployed in everyday life. I referred to Veeran sometime threatening people from whom she was trying to extract money, that she would strip off her clothes and stand naked in front of them. This was experienced as an assault on their own futures as only fearsome goddesses can appear naked and yet unharmed. Scenes of collective violence such as the riots during the Partition of India generated stories of groups of women from the other side being made to march naked to the jeers and insults of men. The whole war of Kurukshetra in the Mahabharata, which leads to the extinction of the Kshatriya race, is seen to originate at the moment when Draupadi is brought to the court of the Kauravas when she is menstruating and Dushasana tries to strip her naked (Das 2013). But Shaikh is not drawing his inspiration from any given theological reflections – he is inventing a theology. As Agamben (2009) argues, nudity bears a theological signature in Western cultures. Being nude and being clothed in the story of Genesis, he says, is not a state but an event. For Shaikh, too, having been made naked is not simply a state of the body but is an event in which the theatre of obscenity enacted in police stations and torture chambers is surrounded with words, curses on the prisoner, threats of not just making him naked but bringing his wife, and sister, and daughter, and mother, and making them naked before his eyes.

It is from within this scene, that the naked body has to be converted from a sign of shame and vulnerability to one of honor and strength. In this way, torture does not affect individual bodies alone.[15] In the sparse biography he provides of his life, and the life of the other accused, he describes his own household – a wife, two children, two younger brothers and their families, mother – then adds within parentheses that his father died when he was in prison because of shock.

Then it happened that one day Wahid called me to check, out of curiosity, if I had read his book in Urdu or in Hindi. As we were talking about the book, I could hear the sound of a woman crying in the background. Not crying in sobs or laments but simply letting out a modulated scream that surged up and receded, in a regular rhythm like rising and falling waves. Wahid explained, "I told the audience when we were at the seminar together at JNU," he said, "my mother has become mentally disturbed. She just cries and she cannot sleep at night." On an impulse I asked if she might want to speak with me, for she was, I felt, participating in our conversation with her cries. And yes, it turned out, she did want to speak with me. I heard Wahid tell his mother, I am his friend from Delhi. We (his mother and I) were now on the phone. I heard a mixture of words and cries. I repeatedly tried to console – your son is home now, why do you cry? I heard a jumble of words, punctuations, hiccups, cries. I was unable to say anything at all. Thinking that I was not there, she asked in a sudden coherent moment, are you there – *aap hain*? "*Haan hun* – yes, I am." Then another moment of coherence – "*Bumbai aana zaroor apne haathon se roti paka ke khilaungi* – you must come to Bombay, I will make food with my own hands to feed you." There is too much to unpack here – making food with her own hands are the sign of the highest intimacy she can offer this stranger whom she learns has befriended her son, who himself has now reemerged in her life after nine years in prison. He is now a trained advocate, an author, and a fierce fighter for abolition of torture. There are others who do not find the language of secular politics or reform adequate. Maulana Geelani, the Muslim leader who has advocated freedom for Kashmir, sent a tweet after the brutal shutdown in Kashmir asking all members of the *ummah* to speak up now or be held as culprits before Allah.

As I put all these expressions and experiences together, I am struck by the multiple layering of forms – intimacy through food, appeals to secular justice, chilling pedagogies of the oppressed, and the language of *ummah*. This form of life is complicated not simply because there are two dimensions – that of form and that of life – but because the soul must find *its* society and *its* own modes of correction in the entanglements of the two. The primitive cry drawn out of Wahid's mother which asserts itself at all kinds of moments is the best example I can give of the enlacing of the social and the natural together in showing how the violence done on one is absorbed by another as inordinate knowledge.

The Third Scene

It is August 2019 in Delhi. I am sitting in Kh's one-room house. Her mother and she have been waiting for me. Kh is excited to show me her schoolwork. The conversation is at first very general but at one point it drifts to the rumors that a girl in the neighborhood has disappeared. According to some people, Kh's mother says, anything from 50 to 70 girls have disappeared from the slums. But she does not know anything about that. Then she says, but I do know a local doctor was involved because he was arrested but he has been released now (*kuch khila pila diya hoga* – placated with food and drink, an obvious reference to bribes). And, she says, I also know the mother of one girl. The girl was recovered from a den of prostitution after she was disappeared. Her mother has refused to register a case with the police because she is scared of the *badnami* – the disrepute. As for me, Kh's mother adds, my daughter has shown such courage that she is now my son – I don't care about the disrepute, and I don't worry about who will marry her – she is now my son.

Kh is in the middle of another story, I guess her fictional double again, who escapes from the clutches of a bad man and returns home. Everyone is happy but her grandfather is very annoyed with her. She hates being in the same room with him – he keeps saying that she should have died – why did she come back? Her mother goes out to work in a factory so it is left to this little girl to provide him his afternoon snacks when she comes back from school but she can never get them in time. . . . The story goes on to describe the many small battles and then the grandfather in the story leaves. I ask where is *your* grandfather today – haven't seen him? She smiles triumphantly and says he has gone and will now live in the village.

Whether Kh, the newly minted son from the degraded body of a daughter, will be able to sustain her ambitions of finishing school, becoming a teacher, looking after her mother as a son would, rather than being packed off to a marital home, are realized in the future or not – I feel something at this moment is precious. Perhaps she will find that her mother can acknowledge her as a daughter which Shanti who figures in *Life and words*, and whose husband and sons were killed in the anti-Sikh violence in 1984 in Delhi, could not as she was constantly reminded that she was now a mother without sons. I still suffer from a feeling of being suffocated when I recall how Shanti's two daughters had come back from school and found her hanging from the ceiling fan and then Babli, saying to me, "when we came back from school, she had done her work." Perhaps this is a different note of resolution, after all.

As the kind of anthropologist that I have become, I am not haunted by big questions such as, given those circumstances would I have become a killer? But other thoughts come unbidden – will I be able to sustain the faith Wahid's mother put in me – will Kh find one helping hand such as mine to be enough? I suspect I will fail.

So, I end with borrowed words: "I am trying to bring out, and keep in balance, two fundamental facts about human forms of life, and about the concepts formed in those forms: that any form of life and every concept integral to it has an indefinite number of instances and directions of projection; and that this variation is not arbitrary" (Cavell 1979: 184). This is an astonishing statement – that human forms of life are plural (there is not simply *a* human condition that remains constant across these forms of life.) The concept of the human, Cavell tells us, could absorb infinite variations and still be recognized through an internal constancy. The minor actors I am so attracted to, and whose actions of care and courage I offer in this book are the only response I am able offer to counter the burden of inordinate knowledge they bear. In those cases, too, there are considerable variations but also an internal consistency.

5
Conclusion:
In Praise of the Minor

I hope the previous chapters have been able to convey that what is at stake in thinking of violence pertains at one level to the character of democracy, of sovereign power, and the way forms of life come to be marked by the violence of the state that seeps into ordinary life. At another level, what is at stake is the question of how the inhuman becomes an eventuality of the human. To ask in what manner is our form of life simultaneously steeped in the milieu defined by the institutions and cultural values we inherit and is also a human form of life is to eschew any ambition to find a prior given, one that will tell us what the human is? What is the scale or range of the human body and the human voice? Rather, it is to let oneself discover what the fate of the human is within the different milieus defined by social and cultural differences but not forced into rigid boundaries. It is also to ask what kind of affordances does a form of life provide which can be used to critique the very institutions we inherit, provided we can let go of the certainties through which we assume we already know where our concepts will take us.

It is particularly striking to me that much theorization

on violence assumes that in order to understand how such stable concepts as state, sovereignty, bureaucracy, technical rationality, subjectivity, or democracy might be empirically tracked, one knows *in advance* where to look. Thus the "natural" place for studying the state is assumed to be *within* the apparatus of the state, such as the bureaucracy or law courts or in the sovereign functions it performs through mechanisms of policing, or lawmaking.[1] One of the arguments I make in this book is that there is no fixed figure and ground relation between a particular social institution and its embodiment – often it is through the traces of the state within the family, or in the everyday events of low-income neighborhoods, that one deciphers certain aspects of the state, its founding and re-founding moments, especially given the episodic character of sovereign power. Sometimes these moments are to be found in documents stored in a family's rusted trunks, sometimes in old wounds on the body, sometimes as part of the habitat emerging over the years and crystallized in jokes, stories, and gestures (see Das and Poole 2004; Han 2013). Even the everyday language used in slums in Delhi which I came to know contained smattering of official language of judges and bureaucrats (e.g., FIR, file, *sunvai* [hearing], warrant, survey), and testified to different kinds of experiences people in these neighborhoods had with the apparatus of the state. Similar to Foucault's characterization of the family as a cell in which one might find intensified forms of sovereign power (Farge and Foucault 2014; Foucault 2003), one can find different cells in different configurations within which sovereign power passes in these neighborhoods. Thus, locating oneself in a slum makes visible certain aspects of what goes on in the higher echelons of the state apparatus in ways that one might not have initially suspected. To recall Dumézil (1988 [1948]) at this point, one could say that there are instances of pact-making aspects of sovereignty visible in the way people negotiate with the police through the mediation of local politicians on the one hand (the Mitra function), and the encounter with force (the Varuna function) when, for instance, arrests are made sporadically to escalate the price (bribe) for release, or at the behest of some local politician to punish certain people. Outside these two poles of sovereignty – that of Mitra and Varuna – the Indra function, the rogue element in sovereignty might be evoked when an event such as the destruction of the Babri mosque, the riots in Mumbai, and the bomb blasts, gets propelled to the national level. In such cases the Indra principle suddenly overtakes the ordinary agreements and the very illegality of these previous pacts becomes the occasion for indiscriminate arrests and police intimidation. I am not claiming that these rogue elements operate only in the slums but the fragility and vulnerability of whole forms of life comes to be staked in such spaces in ways that are perhaps not as readily visible or knowable to wider publics as it is to residents of less secure neighborhoods.[2]

In explaining his own method of doing philosophy through history, Foucault (2008: 3) wrote that he did not start by accepting *a priori* the existence of things like the state, society, the sovereign, and subjects;[3] rather, he arrived at these abstractions through pursuing the traces that concrete people, events, records, left in the archives that made the forms and functions of these institutions visible and intelligible. However, we might ask what happens when you start, not so much with the stance of complete innocence with regard to concepts (as if you had never heard the words state, power, or society before) but by acknowledging an indeterminacy on *where* these are to be found? How could concepts that social scientists use be rethought so as to be seen not as super concepts that belong to some hallowed sites of abstract thought but as humble and quotidian in that they criss-cross with everyday concepts, rather than being ways of carving out the flux of life into domains over which each concept is a master (see Brandel and Motta 2021; Das 2020). As Cavell (2005) said of the inflection of philosophical concepts with ordinary, everyday concepts:

> In his [Wittgenstein's] case, as in the case of the philosophical practice of J.L. Austin, it follows that there are no peculiarly philosophical concepts, none requiring, or entitled to super-ordinary understanding: which in a sense means that there are no ordinary concepts either, none exempt from a philosophical strain. (p. 231)

The concept of inordinate knowledge helped me to see how experiences of violence shaped the physiognomy of words and alerted me to the fact that an attentiveness to minor characters, whether they appeared in court proceedings or police diaries, before disappearing from the records, revealed how they were woven into the textures of the neighborhoods. Perhaps an analogy will help us take some further steps on this line of argument.

In 2009, the literary critic, Alex Woloch, wrote an influential book that upturned the theory of character in the novel by pointing to the readerly interest in secondary characters in literary texts. This interest, he argued, was driven by the tension or even dissonance between the presence (or absence) of the character on the page and its wider influence in the story. As far as the space of the novel is concerned, Woloch (2009) wrote that character spaces do not exist in a vacuum – they are always positioned in relation to each other. Because of the idea that there is an implied personhood behind every actor, the ethical question the reader must ask, he said, is whether there is an obliteration of the person when minor actors are readily expelled from the space of the story.

I am led to ask a similar question. We saw that in the Mumbai train blast terror trials in MCOCA courts, a large number of suspects appeared in the records as the police were trying to put together a narrative of a large conspiracy that involved terrorists from Pakistan and their accomplices from India. Some of the people arrested in this context were coerced into acting as witnesses but a large number were released by the police at different intervals without much explanation, and a large number were eventually acquitted by the courts for lack of evidence. In analogy with the minor characters that Woloch evokes, they disappeared from the page but their large influence in the story is important for us to understand how police tactics of intimidation, physical violence, bribes, and harassment were used to build evidence against suspects the police had picked up on vague suspicions. How do their stories help us understand the tearing of the fabric of relations in the community and the processes through which these relations were repaired, if at all? In this vein, I argued in the second chapter that torture does not act on individual bodies alone but is eminently social in the sense that it draws from deeply embedded textures and nuances of what relationships are. The criteria through which what is honor, what is shame, what is it to be clothed, what is it to be naked, are drawn from forms of life; they are not invented by the police. Yet in using this knowledge within the scene of torture, the torturer destroys the very touch of words, just as the use of everyday objects in torture brings the home into the scene of torture and torture into the scene of the home (Das 2019b; Segal 2020). I gave glimpses of small events around bail applications, or applications submitted to the court to have home-cooked food, medicines, fresh clothes and magazines, delivered to the prisoners.[4] I would like to remind the reader again of Chaganti's (2020) acute observation that what is transpiring in courts is not simply an application to cases of rules picked out from force of habit, but a rearrangement of what are considered to be facts.

I have argued that the final judgment is not the only document through which we can read the unfolding of police procedures. Hence, my claim that the plethora of documents generated in the course of the trial which tend to disappear in dusty archives hold important insights into the coarse and fine grains of the experience of police violence. These insights are important because even highly accomplished anthropologists sometimes claim that it is hard to document physical violence and particularly torture because direct physical violence or incidents of torture do not surface during fieldwork. They find instances of corruption (Jauregui 2017), or humiliation inflicted on members of minorities (Fassin 2013) but for some reason they do not seem to look beyond. For me what this demonstrates is that one has to go beyond the methods of direct observation and be much more attentive to the different kinds of artefacts generated in the course of police work that may not be found in police stations but may well be found in court documents, NGO reports, or through the fieldwork conducted among communities that have been impacted by these police practices. I am not saying that it is not important to consider more subtle forms of moral humil-iation of minorities or immigrants, as demonstrated by Fassin (2013), but to the extent that this discourse slips into claims that Western democracies have over-come "barbaric" or "excessive" forms of violence, it is unfortunate that the close connections between physical and psychological violence are not investigated more directly.[5] What one needs to keep firmly in mind here is that physical injuries, use of technologies such as electric torture, or the administration of narco-analysis[6] is always accompanied with techniques of psychological torture, such as threats to the lives of parents, siblings, spouses, or children of the suspects, which create an atmosphere of terror. The fact that ethnographers can get access to such events only through retrospective testimonies or through court records requires us to think of the methodological perils of trusting only that which we have directly seen or been shown.

As I demonstrated in the TADA cases, after trials that extended over multiple years, a large number of prisoners on trial were acquitted, although the police continued to embroil them in other cases. As recently as this year (2021), a case against 124 Muslims who were arrested for membership of the banned organization SIMI, was dismissed after a period of 19 years and 9 days for serious procedural issues, though the treatment of the prisoners while in custody did not come up in the judgment (*The State of Gujarat* v. *The accused, Ateurrehman Abdul Rehma Qureshi and Others* [Criminal Complaint Numbers, 6497/2002, 3923/2003,20280/2009; judgment 06/03/2021]).[7] It is possible that were it easy to file civil cases for compensation for wrongful confinement in India, more details about the treatment of prisoners would be revealed, but many wrongfully arrested people do not have the resources and do not want to be submitted to continuous police harassment, making it very difficult to bring police abuse to light. This is not, however, an all-or-nothing story, and hence utmost attention needs to be paid to the question of what accounts for the fact that some attentive judges are willing to use legal reasoning to overrule exaggerated claims by investigating authorities, which make small crimes appear as threats to the security and sovereignty of the state; while other judges overlook gross violations of procedure, jurisdiction, and likelihood of forced confessions from the accused through court orders that put those arrested for the flimsiest of reasons at grave risk of police beatings and even torture.

Clean Torture or Torture Without Visible Wounds

Darius Rejali's (2007) monumental study of torture and democracy makes the point that modern torture is based on techniques of inflicting pain that do not leave any mark on the body and that this undermines the legal, medical, and narrative conventions that people count on to express themselves. He avers that victims of such torture by "stealth" are less likely to complain because they cannot prove their injuries as evidence of torture in court. Rejali also concludes that in the absence of visible wounds, it is not only the courts but also members of the victims' own communities who would find it difficult to believe that they were tortured. I will not go into the theory of pain and its expressivity that are the taken-for-granted background of Rejali's claims, but taking a very different stance, Shaikh poses the same problem yet takes the consequences for those being abused in an altogether different direction. In his words:

> Get rid of the notion that the doctor and the court does not know that those under police custody are subjected to third degree torture. The court knows this fact very well, but still courts place the accused in police custody because our courts consider this to be right. Perhaps this notion is present somewhere in the legal domain that unless the accused is tortured, he will not tell the truth about his crime. And thus legal procedures will become ineffective and crime will increase in the country. Now you have to prove that while in police custody you were tortured. But how will you prove this when there are no signs of torture on your body and your medical papers are normal? (Shaikh 2017: 368)

The difficulty that Shaikh identifies is that of having to prove something to the courts which they already know but do not acknowledge. Shaikh assures the second person addressee (here the person who has been tortured and chooses to speak on this in court) that he (Shaikh) is perfectly aware that doctors and judges will dismiss the complaints (they will not believe you, he says) but cites a case where the Supreme Court threw out the confession obtained through coercion under appeal after 12 *years* of litigation in lower courts, because there was a trail of statements made by the prisoner that he was tortured. The striking point here is that corresponding to the long periods of time it takes for courts in India to deliver judgments, Shaikh posits a much longer time horizon for these complaints to come to fruition, but he does not provide any guarantees that they will do so. His only claim is that for an attentive judge to do her work, you, the prisoner have to leave this trail of protests that can be resurrected in the judgment, without which the judge would not have alternatives to draw from.

I contend that Shaikh's words stand in stark opposition to the idea that there are no routes of expression left open in the case of stealth torture or clean torture. It is one thing to say that there are no standing languages[8] with which the experience of torture can be conveyed, and quite another thing to assume that people do not open up new routes of expression, taking what forms of expression they can find in their own forms of life and reshaping them, even distorting them to find expression. There are other cases, for example Shahla Talebi's (2011) courageous work on documenting her own experience of torture in an Iranian prison, which show the work that gestures performed in conjunction with little acts of home-making within the prison – for instance, being able to plant something green on the Iranian New Year – gave expression to the women's defiance of the regime and of the torture inflicted on them to make them into "good" Muslims. Or, for that matter, although the grievous injuries inflicted on Kh did not count as torture according to the legal definition, she found a way to tell her story both in court and through her writing. Her written fiction or memoir is not told in a direct contest with the legal story that cast the policeman as the rescuer and her as the hapless victim, but she found a diagonal route of expression in which she is the major architect of her own freedom. I am not claiming that there is no mismatch between the enormity of suffering and pain imposed on prisoners (and other kinds of captives) who are tortured or subjected to enormous abuse and the expressions they can find, but to judge their forms of expression through some idealized notion of perfect calibration between experience and expression is a further denial of their capabilities (see also Das 1996).

But Rejali and others might still argue, as they do in several places, that there is evidence in victim testimonies and in police and military archives that, because techniques of clean torture, as compared to classical torture, leave no scars or wounds on the body, members of their own communities, in the absence of wounds, find it hard to believe the stories of victims and survivors. But the voices of victims when retrieved from archives in the military, police, and human rights agencies, are structured to make their stories intelligible by making them conform to the judicial picture of victimhood. One can, indeed, find claims in victim testimonies in the archives of human rights organizations of the way relatives and friends abandoned those accused of crimes, or the stigma of being terrorists. But without doubting that many are abandoned, we might want to pay equal attention to those who were shown care (see Mulla 2014). In records produced by lawyers, relatives, and activists that I examined in the cases of terror trials, the relentless effort to get *one more* concession, to get a favorite food to the prisoner, to keep on writing letters full of love even when you knew they would be censored or made into cruel jokes, to get authorization for one more visit, all these acts testify to the fact that families wanted to communicate their care. Moreover, the police do not only target the accused but also use all kinds of methods of cajoling, threatening, enticing of relatives and neighbors, so it is not clear why such communities would believe in the police version of events even when there are no wounds to show.

No Warrant Torture

There is much evidence available now that the specter of terrorism as a threat hanging over the sovereignty of a nation allows police and intelligence agencies to subject many innocent people to torture and illegal confinements, and inhuman punishments (Khan 2008; Slahi 2015). Yet new arguments in defense of the use of torture continue to surface. One of the issues that continues to be discussed after the September 11 terrorist attacks in New York is the question as to whether the nature of terrorist violence would lead one to reconsider justifications for torture to deal with imminent emergencies. The most prominent legal scholar to defend the use of torture, albeit under legal oversight, is surely Alan Dershowitz (2002, 2003), who has argued that his justification for limited use of torture is not about defending torture in general, but defending it only under certain exceptional circumstances. Let us for the moment consider the matter in a cool, deliberative manner without recourse to moral outrage that marks a lot of this discussion on both sides of the debate.

Briefly stated Dershowitz's position is that even though at the normative level torture is reprehensible, most states, including democratic ones, use torture and this fact is an open secret. Under these conditions, he asks, would it not be preferable to bring the practice under judicial scrutiny rather than let it be practiced in secrecy? Dershowitz (and others, e.g., Levinson 2002)[9] call their position one of conditional normativity as the following quotation from Dershowitz (2003) makes clear, but the normative claim then also smuggles into the argument an empirical claim that such judicial review will lead to a reduction of torture since getting a warrant from a judicial or executive authority will make it more difficult to apply torture except in cases of emergency. In his words:

> I then present my conditional normative position, which is the central point of my chapter on torture. I pose the issue as follows: If torture is in fact being used and/or would in fact be used in an actual ticking bomb mass terrorism case, would it be normatively better or worse to have such torture regulated by some kind of warrant, with account-ability, record-keeping, standards, and limitations . . . It is not so much about the substantive issue of torture, as it is over accountability, visibility, and candor in a democracy that is confronting a choice of evils. (pp. 277–8)

I will refrain from commenting on the work that the constant shifts from what are counted as facts and what are counted as norms is doing here, but I do want to bring out some of the hidden assumptions, and some of the facts that are known but pushed out of the frame of the argument. At one level the last sentence in the above quotation is astonishing in that it can simply elide the "substantive" issue of torture – hence all the develop-ments in the technology of torture to which Western democracies have contributed mightily (see Rejali 2007) – and do a balancing act in which accountability, visibil-ity, and candor to save the public culture of democratic politics[10] weighs more heavily on some moral scale than the sheer brutality of torture inflicted on someone defined as a terrorist on the basis of suspicion. As Wisnewski (2008: 315) puts it:

> Dershowitz's case for torture warrants makes heavy use of the worry that not having some sort of judicial review will lead to a nation of hypocrisy. This, it might be objected, misplaces our moral priorities. While it is certainly morally lamentable to engage in hypocrisy, this is hardly comparable to engaging in torture! To suggest, as Dershowitz does, that our hypocrisy is a reason for an open torture policy is, one objection runs, a severe overestimation of the importance of practicing what one preaches.

But returning to the hidden assumptions and relevant facts obliterated in the discussions, let us consider the following issues.

First, narrowing the question of torture to asking if torture would be justified to prevent mass violence has allowed the ticking bomb scenario to take pride of place in these discussions with emphasis on an imminent act of mass violence happening in the near future. At some point in the argument the conditional "if" is converted into a certainty. After all, one might ask how do judges or public officials know that this person under suspicion is the one who has the information to stop the ticking bomb just in time? Since one can only attach probabilities to the likelihood of the police being correct, how much certainty will be required for the warrant to torture to be issued? Is judicial review going to assure that all the prejudices against minorities, racial discrimination, Islamophobia that plague the legal system now will disappear with regard to the person suspected to have the information that only torture will elicit? But then the requirement of urgency within which this thought experiment is framed does not allow for such questions and, at some point, what was conditional slides into what is seen as the factual.

Second, the framing of the thought experiment is in terms of an imminent action happening in the very near future in which time is of the essence. However, most torture happens *retrospectively*, when the police are trying to investigate an event such as a terrorist attack and to frame charges against suspects against whom they do not have enough evidence, or in retaliation for the targeted death of a police officer or attacks on the military (see the report, *Torture: Indian State's Instrument of Control in Indian Administered Jammu and Kashmir* authored by the Association of Parents of Disappeared Persons and Jammu Kashmir Coalition of Civil Society). Although torture is often justified as an attempt to gather information, this information is much more geared toward securing conviction (rather than prevention), establishing conspiracy between those who might otherwise be difficult to connect to each other, and for responding to political pressure to "solve the case." As Rejali (2007) notes, torture done under emergency conditions seems to yield incorrect information because of problems of deception, poor judgment on the part of the interrogators on how to judge the value of the information, and high value placed on information that confirms the suspicions, including prejudices of the police and intelligence officials, rather than yielding anything that would surprise. But who gets to define an emergency given the history of false arrests and intimidation of Muslim suspects in various countries in which terror legislation has been enacted or cases against troublesome minorities such as the Kurdish population in Turkey or Tamils in Sri Lanka?

Third, the assumption of having to choose between two evils singles out *foreign terrorists*, or their domestic accomplices, determined on the basis of religion or ethnicity as the targets of police action. However, torture has been regularly used in disproportionate numbers against minority populations (e.g. African Americans in the United States) in order to obtain, not information, but confessions known to be false but used to legitimize torture by claiming that its techniques yield success. This is the thrust of Laurence Ralph's (2020) book, *The torture letters*, and yet in presenting the case for judicial warrants by its proponents, there is no reference to the impunity with which torture was practiced in cases such as the Area 2 police headquarters under the notorious police sergeant Jon Burge, despite complaints by relatives of African American suspects who had been tortured on the assumption of guilt. G. Flint Taylor, the founding partner of People's Law Office in Chicago, has provided a meticulous account of cases in Area 2, which shows how suppression of evidence, permission to produce falsely obtained confessions in court, and complicity of senior police officials, public prosecutors, as well as judges, was routine in several cases including the case of Andrew Wilson in which he and his brother had been arrested, and false confessions had been extracted under torture (see Taylor 2014). It is particularly salutary to read the key Monell doctrine that was upheld by the court in a subsequent civil rights case filed on behalf of Wilson in 1989, as the judge refused the city's motion to dismiss the case. The judge's words are worth citing:

> [T]here existed in February 1982 in the City of Chicago a de facto policy, practice and/or custom of Chicago Police Officers exacting unconstitutional revenge and punishment against persons who they alleged had injured or killed a fellow officer. This ... revenge and punishment included beating, kicking, torturing, shooting, and/or executing such a person, both for the purpose of inflicting pain, injury and punishment on that person, and also for the purpose

of forcing that person to make an inculpatory statement. (Cited in Taylor 2014: 335)

Andrew Wilson was arrested in 1982 after two white Chicago police officers were shot and killed and Burge was put in charge of the largest manhunt in the city, in which African American neighborhoods were wantonly brutalized. It would take lawyers in People's Law Office several years to get judicial acknowledgment, judges in earlier cases having refused to see the brutalization that was before their eyes. What guarantee would there be, then, that a judicial warrant against foreign terrorists would not participate in the same processes by which police are allowed to suppress information, medical doctors see injuries but do not report them, and judges ignore the evidence before their eyes? In fact, as Ruth Blakeley's (2011) scathing analysis based on the CIA Inspector General's report on enhanced interrogation techniques says, without mincing words:

> I will show that the CIA's deployment of "enhanced interrogation techniques" (EITs), since 2001, constitutes a readoption of Cold War practices tantamount to torture and other cruel, inhuman, and degrading treatment. Their readoption was led by the CIA, and retroactively sanctioned by the OLC under the Bush administration. Furthermore, the CIA initiated harsher measures over time, for which again it retroactively sought permission from the OLC; permission that the OLC granted. In this regard, the tail was wagging the dog; the law was not dictating policy and practice, rather CIA practices were dictating law ... In any case, its use is rarely aimed at thwarting imminent threats, and it is far from clear that it yields any evidence that could not be obtained through legitimate means. (p. 546)

But is anyone listening?

* * *

In writing this book, I have become attuned to the fact that the kind of knowledge one aspires to is shaped by the milieu in which one comes to work, to find one's voice in one's history. But this is a voice carved through its attunement with other voices. Wahid Shaikh's compulsion to write seems a compulsion to leave some traces of his experiences for others to learn from. In an interview he gave to the magazine *Wire*, he recalled that:

> The Mumbai Anti-Terrorism Squad (ATS) arrested me with 12 other accused. The case was totally false and we were arrested in spite of being innocent. We were tortured and beaten up and then we were made to sign confessions forcibly. False witnesses were made up against us. A trial was set up against us in order to punish us. That very moment, I realized that we have been made part of a very huge conspiracy. It was very important to unmask the police who planned such a thing against us. Hence, I made up my mind in 2006 itself that I have to write a book on this issue. I started writing the book in 2006 only but the jail superintendent of Arthur Road jail, Swati Sathe constantly stopped me from writing this book by tearing the pages of my book and at times burned them too. They tried that the book doesn't come out in public.[11]

That the book did get published and that despite the intimidation and the threats he faced, Wahid Shaikh continues to speak, to write, and to inspire others, shows that in addressing questions about violence, anthropology may learn much from different kinds of words it finds companionship with. Whether the accounts I have provided of torture, police procedures, the way what I call inordinate knowledge is absorbed in everyday life, is capable of overcoming the soul blindness in the refusal to acknowledge the facts of torture both inside police stations and outside, I cannot say. I know that I have sometimes been unable to secure such concepts as that of inordinate knowledge. But in becoming the kind of anthropologist I have become, I am wary of boundaries and of closures. I embrace a methodological commitment to ethnography but I also feel that this commitment is not a prison. Learning from a wide range of genres and expressions and methods contained in academic writing, legal judgments, memoirs, data archives, and literary works has given me rare pleasures – above all, the happiness of finding myself among friends who are willing to reach out and offer what help they can give. I am inclined to say that if I have permitted myself some obscurity, I accept that it is a fault of my writing. But it is also, I hope, evidence of my attachment to a concept I cannot fully define and attachment to my interlocutors in what is euphemistically called "the field." Here one might say that it is not specific predicates that define one's concepts; everything one says or does is, or could be, the explanation of one's attachments.

It is my honor that Wahid Shaikh allowed me to dedicate this book to him and his family and I hope the results do not disappoint him.

Notes

1 According to the 2021 Master Plan of Delhi, the unplanned settlements in Delhi can be divided into the following types: resettlement sites, designated slums, urban villages, regularized unauthorized settlements, unauthorized settlements and squatter settlements, also known as JJ (*jhuggi jhopdi*) colonies. Different kinds of settlements enjoy different degrees of security of tenure – so, for instance, designated slums have rights against eviction under the Delhi Slum Act of 1956; resettlement sites that originated under the government's own initiative, most notoriously during the beautification-cum-sterilization drive under the National Emergency in 1976 (Tarlo 2003) gave permanent lease to holders over the land allotted to them. Some squatter settlements might have obtained stay orders against eviction from courts but the possibility of their shanties being demolished always looms over their lives. According to different estimates, about 50–70% of the population of Delhi lives in these "unplanned settlements" – thus these populations are not marginal to the life of the city but constitute its very fabric.

2 Norbert Elias, the scholar whose work on the civilizing process was extremely influential, had to confront the question of Nazi camps at the heart of European civilization and, hence, what was "civilized barbarism." See Elias (1996).

3 For an incisive critique of how the radicalization discourse has been used in the PREVENT strategy in the UK and has achieved discursive popularity though there is little empirical data to support the thesis, see King and Taylor (2011) and Heath-Kelly (2013). For the connection between histories of torture and histories of democracy, see Rejali (2007), Lazreg (2008), and Thénault (2001). Richard Rechtman (2020, 2021) provides a brilliant analysis of questions that extreme violence generates in academic discourse as symptomatic of the ways in which the stakes of engaging this violence come to be centered around the writer's status as a moral person rather than the political conditions of possibility of such violence.

4 On the relation between the order of telling and the order of occurrence, see Goodman (1980, 1981). On the way events get recast as the police officer renders an oral account of a complaint into a document recognizable to the law, see Satyogi (2019).

5 See Das (1977, 1985) for an account of how other Sanskrit texts such as the Puranas acknowledge the rogue or evil aspect hidden in kingship and the role of cleansing rituals during the coronation of the king.

6 The three domains making up the pattern are, in descending order of value: sovereignty with its magical and juridical aspects and a sort of maximal expression of the sacred; physical force and valor, whose most salient manifestation is victorious warfare; and fecundity and prosperity, with more complications than I can enumerate here (see Dumézil 1958; see also Hiltebeitel 1974). It is beyond the scope of this discussion, but I point to the fact that Indra commits

all three sins of the warrior in the realm of each of the functions (Dubuisson 1986) and each time one of his attributes leaves him for another deity. This is what makes it hard to treat Vedic deities as stable entities and to fully endorse Dumézil's understanding of the function of gods in Vedic sacrifice that he took from Marcel Mauss.

7 Krishna also displays extraordinary compassion at the moment when he saves Draupadi from the humiliation of being made naked in the court of Dhritarashtra after her husband, Yudhishthira, has used her as stake in a bet with Duryodhana that he loses. As Dushasana, one of the Kaurava brothers tries to disrobe her, Krishna magically extends her sari to a never-ending length till Dushasana has to give up. Draupadi then takes the vow to leave her hair loose and wild till she can anoint it with the blood taken from the broken thigh of Dushasana, the same thigh on which he had invited her to sit naked. Draupadi's affinity to the figure of the avenging Kali becomes evident here.

8 I realized how little attention has been paid to the question of sexuality within sovereignty when I read Moore's learned commentary on Deleuze and Guattari's interpretation of the "third persona," the warrior or nomad "who is unable to serve any one (or two) images because s/he is subject to too broad a range of affect or perception: one who bears too much" (Moore 2012: 139). Let us note that the simple alternative suggested here by the use of *s/he* shows the indifference on the part of Moore to parse out what is it stake in the warrior function being invested in *Indra* with his rogue sexuality and the difference in thinking of the warrior function through one of the war goddesses on which Dumézil did not gain clarity. If, indeed, Dumézil could be taken to read that the power of Indra is ensnared within the two poles of the sovereign, surely a war goddess with all her

disguises and ruses could not have been ensnared in the same manner. As if matters were not difficult enough, Maunaguru's (2020) excellent formulation as to how the LTTE (Tamil Tigers) challenged Sri Lankan political sovereignty, establishing their own laws in the territories it controlled, but could not challenge the sovereignty of the established deities of Tamil temples in the same region, shows the tremendous challenges of understanding the relation between the warrior function and the two-headed sovereignty of Mitra and Varuna. As an aside, one might also consider how new kinds of urban warfare have led to a folding of the warrior into the professional soldier even in modern armies (see Barry 2008).

9 "[G]iven that three points define a circle and that we already know that a circle – as well as being the name for a group of people sharing an interest – is for Emerson another figure for an essay, I would say that Emerson is here conceiving the origin of an essay as the conversation of the circle of figures by which it has been inspired" (Cavell 2005, 132).

10 Diamond makes it clear in at least two end notes that she is not denying a role to argument but is pointing to the contexts in which argument simply becomes a form of avoidance of the real issues at stake.

11 TADA is the abbreviation for the Terrorist and Disruptive Activities (Prevention) Act which was in force between 1985 and 1995.

Chapter 2: The Catastrophic Event: Enduring Inordinate Knowledge

1 According to the charge sheet filed in the special court of Justice J.N. Patel, charges were filed against 128 persons, two accused were dead by the time the charges were filed, and 31 (including some Pakistani nationals) absconded.

2 The Babri Masjid, a sixteenth-century mosque in

Ayodhya considered in the Hindu traditions to be the birthplace of Rama, was part of a lengthy legal dispute, going back to 1859, on whether it had been built on the site of a demolished Rama temple, with both Muslims and Hindus claiming exclusive rights to worship there (see Mehta 2015, 2018). The final judgment on the dispute was given by the Supreme Court on November 9, 2019, though the mosque had already been illegally demolished by activists of the Vishva Hindu Parishad and allied organizations aligned with the Hindu right Bharatiya Janata Party (BJP). The Supreme Court in its final judgment converted the dispute to one over property and adverse possession, rather than right to worship, but the judgment was seen by many to be deeply flawed.

3 See Brooks (2000) for discussion of court cases in the US in which confessions secured by police through false statements or implicit threats made to the accused were nevertheless considered sufficient for conviction. Confession, as Brooks says, is regarded as the most authentic of proofs, even apparently when the suspect was willing to confess to anything to escape police pressure. See also Taylor (2009) for a discussion of the different genres of confession.

4 The Students' Islamic Movement of India was deemed to be a terrorist organization and was banned in 2001, after the September 11 attacks in the US. The ban has been renewed several times, the latest being in February 2019.

5 Covid-19 and subsequent severe illness interrupted my plans to gather more documentation on these trials.

6 I have not attempted any comparisons across similar accounts written by others partly because I want to bring attention to the work that texts written in vernacular languages are able to achieve, but I feel beholden to the activist lawyers and human rights workers, who have worked with those falsely accused

in terror cases to develop their memoirs for English-speaking readers (see, for instance, Khan and Haksar 2016).

7 All translations from Hindi to English are mine.

8 Tobias Kelly (2011) has shown how difficult it is to establish the connection between bruises and torture in courts even under the UN's well-intentioned *Istanbul Protocol: Manual on the Effective Investigation and Documentation of Torture and Other Cruel, Inhuman, or Degrading Treatment or Punishment* (1999).

9 The police often use the term "routine questioning" when picking up suspects, not only in terror-related cases but also for petty crimes. See, for instance, Gautam and Gautam (2014) from the NGO, Society for Environment, Health, Awareness of Nutrition & Toxicology (SEHAT), which documents torture-related deaths in police custody of people arrested for petty crimes in the city of Meerut in Uttar Pradesh.

10 For an erudite discussion of the metaphysics of nothingness in the Indic traditions and the controversies internal to Indian philosophy of these issues, see Billimoria (2012). Any further consideration of these issues that span theories of ritual hermeneutics, grammar, and logic in Brahmanical, Buddhist, and Jain sources would take us far from the scope of this chapter and my competence in these matters is limited. Nevertheless, I regret very much the artificial wall between Western philosophy and the philosophies of the East.

11 See the excellent analysis by Serra Hakyemez (2016) of Kurdish terror trials in Turkish courts, and the judicial reasoning through which ordinary crimes are converted into terrorist acts.

12 "Victory to Lord Rama" has become a badge or, a sound bite, of some Hindus using it militantly to threaten Muslims in public spaces, similar to the way *Allah-O-Akbar* and *Jay Ma Bhavani* – Allah is Great

and Victory to the Goddess – were slogans used in riots during the Partition of India by Muslims and Hindus respectively.

Chapter 3: *The Dispersed Body of the Police and Fictions of the Law*

1 On the role of such little tools of knowledge in creating the impression of authoritative discourse, see Becker and Clark (2001).

2 I have discussed this case in detail elsewhere (see Das 2020: ch. 8) but in this earlier discussion I focused on what transpired in court and paid much more attention to features of legal language that revealed how one is made the subject of law, the split between one who has experienced violence and one who has witnessed it in the same person, as well as the judge expressing agency from a distance. For several reasons, I had to defer an analysis of the kind of talk it generated in the neighborhood. Here I need to reproduce some of the material from my earlier essay, but I hope that by bringing in the milieu of the slum more frontally into the analysis I will be able to pay more attention to other aspects, especially on how the event secretes knowledge which is not allowed to surface in the court.

3 For example, it is assumed that First Information Reports (FIRs) are dictated by the policeman on duty to the person who comes in with a complaint. For examples, see Das (2007) on the framing sentences in FIRs filed in police stations by victims of riots. See also Satyogi (2019) for the process of converting oral complaints into written documents in police stations.

4 Courts tend not to use the term torture in rape trials, though there are clear similarities in the manner in which harm is inflicted on the body between what happens in torture rooms in prisons and what happens to women forcibly confined. The difference is that in police stations care is taken to see that injuries inflicted

do not leave a mark on the body so as to avoid being read as evidence. The legal definition of torture as cruel or inhuman pain inflicted by a public official, while important for jural purposes, leaves open the question of torture in domestic spaces.

5 The masculine marker is used in the verb, perhaps because the petition was typed at a small store in the nearby market, by someone not too skilled in typing.

6 See Clara Han's (2013) fascinating discussion of how the police deployed in the neighborhoods characterized by drug wars in Santiago, Chile, came to be seen as being somewhere between strangers and proximate kin. For instance, a mother unable to control the violence of an adult son might turn to a policeman to control her son; but at other moments regard him as the enemy bringing destruction to the neighborhood. Similarly, Pooja Satyogi shows how women police officers take on the voice of mediation in the counselling role they are asked to play with regard to women who come to report domestic violence but interpret what constitutes domestic violence in very broad terms (see especially Satyogi 2019).

7 The conversations go like this: *"aap ko to pata hai, mahaul kitna kharab hai yahan ka"*; *"ladkiyon ka kahin aana jaana bhi mushkil ho jaata hai"*; *"aapko pata hai ham kisi se matlab nahin rakhte,"* *"aapko pata hair hum to apne kaam se matlab rakhte hain."*

8 See the layers of ethnographic knowledge through which Singh (2015) reveals the varied roles and different voices one of his most memorable respondents, Kali, embodies as a human rights worker, as a member of a local NGO, as a woman in an intimate relation with a *jinn*, as one integrated in her husband's lineage and also alienated from it, as a minor political figure in local disputes.

9 The conceptual proximity between gift and bribe has been noted by many scholars who write on corruption

and the moral ambiguities surrounding this term (see Das 2015; de Sardan 1999; Humphrey 2021).

10 *"File daba di"* – the file was disappeared is part of the work that police perform before a case reaches the courts, as some people explained to me. But one's own lawyer might also be bribed to do so. In the next chapter, I discuss the lethal consequences of these practices through which many innocent people are framed and charged with serious crimes. In the case of Kh, we saw that the practice was not benign but then, one has to see this expression in tandem with other threats such as *jhuthe case mein phasana* – to embroil someone in a false case. At the local level the police might also act as arbiters of deciding who might be guilty and who might be innocent on the basis of local knowledge they have of the area.

Chapter 4: Detecting the Human: Under Which Skies Do We Theorize?

1 Simpson (2012) makes an important claim in interpreting Foucault's turn to *parrhesia* when he writes: "Foucault appears to advocate a practice of truthful speech, while also being committed, as many commentators have shown, to the project of showing truth to be produced, intermeshed with power relations, and situated. Foucault constructively works through this latter problem by admitting that truth is ultimately fictional, though not merely so: 'fictions' are productive of bodies, pleasures, selves, and power relations which themselves produce other truths. In this framework, *parrhesia* would not only be truthful engagement with others, but the constructive telling of fictions to both oneself and others that would produce the effects of truth" (p. 100). I invite the reader to forge connections between this interpretation of effects of truth with effects that fictions of law have for arriving at a judicial truth conducive to justice in attentive judgments.

2 These are ritual recitations of "There is none worthy of worship except God (Allah) and Muhammad is the messenger of God." The recitation of *darood sharif* is to send blessings upon the Prophet.

3 ISERDD refers to a research and advocacy organization that has worked over the past several years in the slums of Delhi to support health and education initiatives, and to provide support to individuals in precarious conditions.

4 A literal translation of *bhayanak* is one who exudes terror, or one who can make your heart jittery and full of apprehension, one who creates fear. I think evil might capture the affect behind all these meanings, if we remember its usage in fairy tales (the evil fairy) or in folk tales (the bad wolf), rather than in theology.

5 This is not to say that we have not seen amazing experiments with genre as these emerge in literature, theatre, and film (think of writers like Delbo 2014; Kang 2017; Khoury 2015; Manto 2008) but that to expect to get a realistic picture of what such experiences of violence meant for the victims and the perpetrators requires one to forgo certainties, which at least the social science literature is not ready to do. Still, it is not an all-or-nothing game and I feel very beholden to those who keep trying to pose new questions and recognize that a certain disappointment with oneself is the price of dealing with such issues.

6 I do not wish to claim that all forms of reconciliation are to be treated as suspect, as from my own experiences in India I know the heterogeneity and unpredictability of human desires and capabilities. I have witnessed the exhaustion of hatred as much as the exhaustion of love; and some of my work shows how even within nationalist projects relationships can come to acquire new and different meanings than those projected on people by institutions of the State (Das 2007).

7 Storytelling and giving verbal testimonies are important

but outside of the structures of crime and punishment, there are also other ways in which inordinate knowledge is absorbed though never fully mastered as, for instance, through rituals, through small acts of care, that allow life to be knitted back pair by pair, so to speak (see Cavell 1996). The texture of the ordinary does not erase the traces of violence, nor necessarily do people simply forgive and reconcile, but as Donatelli (2019) says, a form of life however sublime, however degraded is still a form of life for those who inhabit it. See the excellent work on different routes for the return to the ordinary by Çelik (2020), Giellou (2015), Han (2020), Han and Brandel (2020), Kwon (2006, 2008), Rojas-Perez (2017), among others. See also Das (2007, 2021) and Han (2020) for an extraordinary rendering of the way violence and care are knitted in the familial relations through the voice of the child.

8 Rechtman writes: "As horrific as this practice is, in no way does it sum up the quotidian crimes committed during the four years of the Khmer Rouge regime. And even if its legend, from a distance, seems to exceed its actual scope by far, as it becomes sometimes a subject of conversation between the Khmer Rouge and then between survivors, it has never occupied an essential place in the most personal accounts of former killers. This killing practice, in other words, is simply not what genocidaires speak or write of, to their families. Instead, they recount their quotidian lives: small torments, simple details, lack of amusement, the anger of their immediate bosses, annoyances at their colleagues, and the rare moments of glory when a superior bestowed congratulations or encouragements. These moments are trivial and insignificant; they are of little interest to the grand history of the age" (p. 132).

9 *hamare friend's circle mein ye custom ban gaya hai . . .*

10 "Outside" here refers to food eaten in a relatively cheap restaurant or *dhaba* in one of the local markets.

11 Based on this legend, the Tamil film *Chitoor Rani Padmini* was shown in 1963 and a Hindi film *Rani Padmini* in 1964.

12 See Chatterjee (2018), Gehlawat (2019), and Qureshi (2018) for further discussion on the controversies around the film in popular culture and its implications for varied topics such as nationalism, masculinity, and the relation between aesthetics and politics.

13 I am not going into this issue in greater detail here but events such as the passing of the Citizenship Amendment Bill in 2019 and the abrogation of Article 370 of the Constitution that gave a separate legal status to Jammu and Kashmir have rightly been seen as grievous blows to the secular project in India.

14 That these two different kinds of possibilities refer to different modalities of absence has been a point made in many philosophies including in Kant and in Nyaya philosophy.

15 See especially Lotte Buch Segal (2018) on how the experience of torture spills into the family.

Chapter 5: Conclusion: In Praise of the Minor

1 I do not rehearse the well-plowed discussion of sovereignty and political theology as in Schmitt (2005), but note that Kahn (2011) already shows the departures from the general model proposed by Schmitt for the case of the United States in which the valorization of sacrifice as a supreme religious duty toward the nation troubles Schmitt's categories. The new war theories that now consider non-state actors to have largely replaced the emphasis on state-constituted armies are important but largely overlook the central role played by states in fueling so-called civil violence or for that matter in the investment of states in supporting terrorism in one way or another (see Das 2008; Halliday 2001; Schuurman 2010).

2 I have been asked several times whether the conditions

I describe are particular to the slums or can these be generalized for other populations? Of course, the poor are not the only ones who live on illegally occupied land or who manipulate electric bills. The residents of more secure neighborhoods also make unauthorized extensions to their houses or shops, engage in underhand transactions, hold stacks of black money and sometimes they, too, come into the grips of the law, but a comparison is not the purpose of this book. It is to draw attention to the specificity of the risks and perils to which life in the slums and in low-income neighborhoods is particularly exposed.

3 While I cannot develop the thought in great detail here, I want to, at the very least, gesture toward the resonance with the well-known Buddhist debates on the character of conceptual wholes created through language whose reality is seen as confined to the conventional reality of social life but to which the ontological commitment was of a different order than the ontological commitment to the parts into which a whole could be broken to generate new material objects.

4 Punathil (2020) makes a nice case for considering archives as ethnographic sites, not as spaces for knowledge retrieval but of knowledge creation, following the classic work of Stoler (2010). Punathil shows the importance of genre in casting conflict across different kinds of communities in courts and in commissions of inquiry within a dominant paradigm of Hindu–Muslim conflict in India. I have found it useful to think of the plot structure that emerges in forced confessional statements through the concept of the chronotope.

5 The very claim that psychological techniques such as sleep deprivation, or the claim that waterboarding only produced a feeling of suffocation and drowning and hence constituted enhanced interrogation but

not torture, is the typical obfuscation through which extensive use of torture is reclassified as civilized, rather than brute violence. See Wolfendale (2009) for a stinging critique of such claims, in addition to Rejali (2007).

6 Narco-analysis refers to the use of "truth serum," injectable sodium pentothal in criminal investigations along with the use of lie detectors and brain scans. Collectively referred to as deception detection tests, the use of narco-analysis has come under heavy criticism from human rights advocates in India. The Supreme Court of India has held that such tests cannot be administered without securing consent from the accused. For an excellent discussion on the so-called "truth machines," see Lokaneeta (2020). The use of such techniques has been defended primarily on the ground that it is better than third-degree torture as in M. S. Rao (2006) and Tyagi (2019).

7 As many defense lawyers would concede, the imperative before them in such cases is to find ways of securing acquittal and if this requires that they do not bring up the treatment accorded to the client while in custody, this is a compromise they might need to make. In Kh's case, for example, the threats made by the police against her parents were not ever consolidated as a complaint once the case reached the court.

8 The concept of standing language was famously articulated by Cavell in relation to the problem of knowing the pain of the other. The absence of standing languages was part of the grammar of pain, he said, and related it to skepticism as a standing threat that lines the everyday and against which you are allowed to neither win nor lose. In his comment on my reflections on pain, he spoke of the absence of standing or given languages making it necessary to beg, borrow, steal, or invent new words or tones of words in order to break

the silence on pain (Cavell 1979, 1996). See also Das (1996, 2007, 2020).

9 Levinson's (2002) essay is a very good example of writing in which one suspects that the problem is not that there is no escape *from* philosophy in such morally fraught discussions but that there is a ready escape *to* philosophy as in his admiring evocation of Michael Walzer's ingenious equivalence of the pain inflicted on a victim under dubious circumstances with suitable guilt on the part of those "otherwise" decent political figures who authorize it. For instance, Levinson assumes that there must surely be some instances in which torture succeeds in extracting information from the victim but elides how many people must be tortured to get information from one, even if some information is extracted. Here is a telling quote: "Instead, I believe that one must accept some version of the view articulated by Michael Walzer in his classic essay, 'The problem of dirty hands', where he explicitly endorses the necessity of having political leaders who are willing, in dire circumstances, to engage in quite horrendous actions, including torture, though their saving grace, if that is the right word, is feeling suitably guilty about violating what most people indeed wish were an 'absolute' prohibition" (p. 2032). See Blakeley (2011) for a detailed account of the CIA Inspector General's report on the inefficacy of "enhanced interrogation techniques," but in some versions of legal theory, one must never allow facts to interfere with a theory from an essay regarded as a classic or expect corrections to facts one had presupposed, which turn out to be based on no evidence at all. See also Allen (2005).

10 Although some distinguished anthropologists have found resemblances between a political culture of one-party rule, authoritarianism, and attribution of misfortunes and adverse outcomes of policy to occult powers with a culture of witchcraft accusations

(Geschiere 1997, among others), one wonders why they are less inclined to take up the political culture of democratic societies in which the false confessions secured through torture techniques are taken as evidence of the success of the draconian methods of investigation, legal or not. Anthropologists also turn to Austin (1962) to ask what the felicity conditions are under which speech acts generated as evidence of conspiracy theories come to be seen as true (Fassin 2021). However attractive such a move may seem at first sight, it fails to register the contrast between felicity conditions of speech acts with illocutionary force and those with perlocutionary force – thus obscuring the fact that in the former case the context is determined by convention whereas in the latter case access to context is extremely fragile and hence felicity conditions are not easy to specify (see Das 2020).

11 See "Interview: Of torture, impunity and the false charges on Abdul Wahid Shaikh," https://thewire.in/law/abdul-wahid-shaikh-acquitted-interview.

References

Agamben, Giorgio. 1991. *Language and death: The place of negativity.* Minneapolis: University of Minnesota Press.

Agamben, Giorgio. 1998. *Homo sacer: Sovereign power and bare life* (tr. Daniel Heller-Roazan). Stanford, CA: Stanford University Press.

Agamben, Giorgio. 2009. *Nudités.* Paris: Bibliothèque Rivages.

Ahmad, Irfan. 2017. "Injustice and the new world order: An anthropological perspective on 'terrorism' in India." *Critical Studies on Terrorism* 10.1: 115–37.

Ahmad, Nehaluddin, and Gary Lilienthal. 2016. "Proscribing torture: An analysis in Indian and ethical contexts (The 2010 Indian Prevention of Torture Bill)." *Commonwealth Law Bulletin* 42.1: 38–58.

Allen, Jonathan. 2005. "Warrant to torture?: A critique of Dershowitz and Levinson." ACDIS Occasional Papers.

Allen, Nicholas J. 1999. "Arjuna and the second function: A Dumézilian crux." *Journal of the Royal Asiatic Society* 9.3: 403–18.

Arendt, Hannah. 1963. *Eichmann in Jerusalem: A report on the banality of evil.* New York: Viking Press.

Asad, Talal. 2007. *On suicide bombing*. New York: Columbia University Press.

Asad, Talal. 2010. "Thinking about terrorism and just war." *Cambridge Review of International Affairs* 23.1: 3–24.

Austin, John Langshaw. 1946. "Other minds." *Proceedings of the Aristotelian Society, Supplementary Volume* S20: 148–87.

Austin, John Langshaw. 1962. *How to do things with words*. Cambridge, MA: Harvard University Press.

Austin, Jonathan Luke. 2016. "Torture and the material-semiotic networks of violence across borders." *International Political Sociology* 10: 3–21.

Bakhtin, Mikhail. 1982. *The dialogic imagination: Four essays* (tr. Caryl Emerson and Michael Holquist). Austin: University of Texas Press.

Bargu, Banu. 2021. "Authority." In *Words and worlds: A lexicon for dark times* (eds. Veena Das and Didier Fassin). Durham, NC: Duke University Press, 61–82.

Barry, John Christopher. 2008. "Vaincre l'ennemi ou le détruire? *American warrior*." *Inflexions* 2: 175–94.

Baxi, Upendra. 2005. "The 'war on terror' and the 'war of terror': Nomadic multitudes, aggressive incumbents and the 'new' international law: prefatory remarks on two 'wars'." *Osgoode Hall Law Journal* 43.1–2: 7–43.

Becker, Peter, and William Clark, eds. 2001. *Little tools of knowledge: Historical essays on academic and bureaucratic practices*. Ann Arbor: University of Michigan Press.

Benjamin, Walter. 2019 [1978]. "Critique of violence." In *Reflections: Essays, aphorisms, autobiographical writings* (ed. Peter Demetz). New York: Harcourt Mifflin, 291–316.

Billimoria, Purshottam. 2012. "Why is there nothing rather than something? An essay in the comparative metaphysic of nonbeing." *Sophia* 51: 509–30.

Blakeley, Ruth. 2011. "Dirty hands, clean conscience?

The CIA Inspector General's investigation of 'enhanced interrogation techniques' in the war on terror and the torture debate." *Journal of Human Rights* 10.4: 544–61.

Bourdieu, Pierre. 1990. *The logic of practice*. Stanford, CA: Stanford University Press.

Brandel, Andrew, and Marco Motta. 2021. *Living with concepts: Anthropology in the grip of reality*. New York: Fordham University Press.

Brooks, Peter. 2000. *Troubling confessions: Speaking guilt in law and literature*. Chicago, IL: University of Chicago Press.

Cavell, Stanley. 1979. *The claim of reason: Wittgenstein, skepticism, morality, and tragedy*. Oxford: Oxford University Press.

Cavell, Stanley. 1996. "Comments on Veena Das's essay: Language and body: Transactions in the construction of Pain." *Daedalus* 125.1: 93–8.

Cavell, Stanley. 2005. *Philosophy the day after tomorrow*. Cambridge, MA: Harvard University Press.

Cavell, Stanley. 2007a. "Companionable thinking." In *Wittgenstein and the moral life: Essays in honor of Cora Diamond* (ed. Alice Crary). Cambridge, MA: The MIT Press, 281–8.

Cavell, Stanley. 2007b. "Foreword." In *Life and words* (Veena Das). Berkeley: University of California Press.

Cavell, Stanley. 2008. "Companionable thinking." In *Philosophy and animal life* (Stanley Cavell, Cora Diamond, John McDowell, Ian Hacking, and Cary Wolfe). New York: Columbia University Press, 91–126.

Cavell, Stanley. 2010. "The touch of words." In *Seeing Wittgenstein anew* (eds. William Day and Victor J. Krebs). Cambridge: Cambridge University Press, 81–100.

Çelik, Önder. 2020. *Life underground: Hunting for Armenian treasure in a post-genocide landscape*. Unpublished dissertation, Johns Hopkins University.

Chaganti, Sruti, 2020. "Two genealogies of the juridical: Fact and ruse". Unpublished manuscript.

Chatterjee, Partha. 2018. "Women and nation revisited." *South Asian History and Culture* 9.4: 380–7.

Coetzee, J. M. 2003. *Elizabeth Costello*. London: Secker & Warburg.

Das, Veena. 1977. *Structure and cognition: Aspects of Hindu caste and ritual.* Delhi: Oxford University Press.

Das, Veena. 1985. "Paradigms of body symbolism: An analysis of selected themes in Hindu culture." In *Indian religion* (ed. Richard Burghart, and Audrey Cantlie). London: Curzon Press, 180–207.

Das, Veena. 1996. "Language and body: Transactions in the construction of pain." *Daedalus* 125.1: 67–91.

Das, Veena. 2007. *Life and words: Violence and the descent into the ordinary.* Berkeley: University of California Press.

Das, Veena. 2008. "Collective violence and the shifting categories of communal riots, ethnic cleansing and genocide." In *The historiography of genocide* (ed. Dan Stone). London: Palgrave Macmillan, 93–127.

Das, Veena. 2011. "State, citizenship, and the urban poor." *Citizenship Studies* 15.3–4, 319–33.

Das, Veena. 2013. "Violence and nonviolence at the heart of Hindu ethics." *The Oxford handbook of religion and violence* (eds. Michael Jerryson, Mark Juergensmeyer, and Margo Kitts). New York: Oxford University Press, 15–40.

Das, Veena. 2014. "Action, expression, and everyday life: Recounting household events." In *The ground between: Anthropologists engage philosophy* (eds. Veena Das, Michael D. Jackson, Arthur Kleinman, and Bhrigupati Singh). Durham, NC: Duke University Press, 279–306.

Das, Veena. 2015. "Corruption and the possibility of life." *Contributions to Indian Sociology* 49.3: 322–43.

Das, Veena. 2019a. "A child disappears: Law in the courts,

law in the interstices of everyday life." *Contributions to Indian Sociology* 53.1: 97–132.

Das, Veena. 2019b. "Where is democracy in India? Asking anthropological theory to open its doors." Anthropological Theory Commons blogpost. Available at: https://www.at-commons.com/2019/11/24/where-is-democracy-in-india-asking-anthropological-theory-to-open-its-doors/.

Das, Veena. 2020. *Textures of the ordinary: Doing anthropology after Wittgenstein.* New York: Fordham University Press.

Das, Veena. 2021. "Knowledge." In *Words and worlds: A lexicon for dark times* (eds. Veena Das and Didier Fassin). Durham, NC: Duke University Press, 19–38.

Das, Veena, and Deborah Poole. 2004. *Anthropology in the margins of the state: Comparative ethnographies.* Santa Fe, NM: School of American Research Press.

Das, Veena, and Shalini Randeria. 2015. "Politics of the urban poor: Aesthetics, ethics, volatility, precarity." *Current Anthropology* 56.S11: S3–S14.

Das, Veena, and Michael Walton. 2015. "Political leadership and the urban poor: Local histories." *Current Anthropology* 56.S1: S44–S54.

de Sardan, J. P. Olivier. 1999. "A moral economy of corruption in Africa?" *The Journal of Modern African Studies* 37.1: 25–52.

De Waal, Alex. 2015. *The real politics of the Horn of Africa: Money, war and the business of power.* Chichester: John Wiley & Sons.

De Waal, Alex. 2021. "Power." In *Words and worlds: A lexicon for dark times* (eds. Veena Das and Didier Fassin). Durham, NC: Duke University Press, 123–42.

Del Mar, Maksymilian, and William Twining, eds. 2015. *Legal fictions in theory and practice.* New York: Springer.

Delbo, Charlotte. 2014. *Auschwitz and after.* New Haven, CT: Yale University Press.

Deleuze, Gilles, and Félix Guattari. 1987. *A thousand plateaus: Capitalism and schizophrenia* (tr. Brian Massumi). Minnesota: Minnesota University Press.

Dershowitz, Alan M. 2002. *Why terrorism works: Understanding the threat, responding to the challenge.* New Haven, CT: Yale University Press.

Dershowitz, Alan M. 2003. "The torture warrant: A response to Professor Strauss." *NYLS Law Review* 48: 275–94.

Diamond, Cora. 2001. "The case of the naked soldier." *Cités* 1: 113–25.

Diamond, Cora. 2003. "The difficulty of reality and the difficulty of philosophy." *Partial Answers: Journal of Literature and the History of Ideas* 1.2: 1–26.

Diamond, Cora. 2008. "The difficulty of reality and the difficulty of philosophy." In *Philosophy and animal life* (Stanley Cavell, Cora Diamond, John McDowell, Ian Hacking & Cary Wolfe). New York: Columbia University Press, 43–90.

Diop, Boubacar Boris. 2006. *Murambi: The book of bones.* Bloomington: Indiana University Press.

Donatelli, Piergiorgio. 2019. "The social and the ordinary." *Iride* 32.86: 441–55.

Dubuisson, Daniel. 1986. *La légende royale dans l'Inde ancienne: Rāma et le Rāmāyana.* Paris: Éditions Economica.

Dumézil, Georges. 1958. *L'ldéologie tripartite des Indo-européens.* Brussels: Latomus.

Dumézil, Georges. 1988 [1948]. *Mitra-Varuna: An essay on two Indo-European representations of sovereignty.* New York: Zone Books.

Elias, Norbert. 1996. *The Germans.* Cambridge: Polity.

Farge, Arlette and Michel Foucault. 2014. *Le désordre des familles.* Paris: Gallimard.

Farooqui, Mahmood. 2019. Review: Begunah Qaidi by Abdul Wahid Sheikh. *Hindustan Times*, August 24. Available at: https://www.hindustantimes.com/books/

review-begunah-qaidi-by-abdul-wahid-sheikh/story-oEy
ey5ozNTotgoxJLUXMxK.html

Fassin, Didier. 2013. *Enforcing order: An ethnography of urban policing*. London: Polity.

Fassin, Didier. 2017. *Prison worlds: An ethnography of the carceral condition*. London: John Wiley & Sons.

Fassin, Didier. 2021. "Of plots and men: The heuristics of conspiracy theories." *Current Anthropology* 62.2: 128–137.

Foucault, Michel. 1990. *Maurice Blanchot: The thought from outside*. New York: Zone Books.

Foucault, Michel, 2003. *Society must be defended: Lectures at the Collège de France, 1975–1976* (ed. François Ewald). London: Macmillan.

Foucault, Michel. 2006. *Psychiatric power: Lectures at the Collège de France, 1973–1974* (tr. Graham Burchell). New York: Palgrave Macmillan.

Foucault, Michel. 2008. *The birth of biopolitics: Lectures at the Collège de France 1978–1979* (tr. Graham Burchell). New York: Palgrave Macmillan.

Foucault, Michel. 2011. *The courage of truth; The government of self and others II: Lectures at the Collège de France, 1983–1984* (tr. Graham Burchell). New York: Palgrave Macmillan.

Gautam, Sarla, and Aaju Gautam. 2014. "Victim of torture in police custody: A case study." *International Journal of Higher Education and Research* 5.1, 1–8.

Gehlawat, Ajay. 2019 "Triumph of the Rajput: Sanjay Leela Bhansali and the fascist aesthetics of Padmaavat." *Studies in South Asian Film & Media* 9.2: 159–72.

Geschiere, Peter. 1997. *The modernity of witchcraft: Politics and the occult in postcolonial Africa*. Charlottesville: University of Virginia Press.

Ghassem-Fachandi, Parvis. 2012. *Pogrom in Gujarat: Hindu nationalism and anti-Muslim violence in India*. Princeton, NJ: Princeton University Press.

Giellou, Anne Yvonne. 2015. "Traces of destruction and the thread of continuity in post-genocide Cambodia." In *Living and dying in the contemporary world: A compendium* (eds. Veena Das and Clara Han). Berkeley: University of California Press, 729–42.

Goodman, Nelson. 1980. "Twisted tales; Or, story, study, and symphony." *Critical Inquiry* 7.1: 103–19.

Goodman, Nelson. 1981. "The telling and the told." *Critical Inquiry* 7.4: 799–801.

Gros, Frédéric. 2011. "Course summary." In *The courage of truth; The government of self and others II: Lectures at the Collège de France, 1983–1984* (Michel Foucault). New York: Palgrave Macmillan.

Guha, Ranajit. 2002. *History at the limit of world-history.* New York: Columbia University Press.

Hacking, Ian. 2008. "Deflections." In *Philosophy and animal life* (Stanley Cavell, Cora Diamond, John McDowell, Ian Hacking & Cary Wolfe). New York: Columbia University Press, 139–172.

Hakyemez, Serra M. 2016. *Lives and times of militancy: Terrorism trials, state violence and Kurdish political prisoners in post-1980 Turkey.* Unpublished dissertation, Johns Hopkins University.

Halliday, Fred. 2001. "The romance of non-state actors." In *Non-state actors in world politics* (eds. Daphné Josselin and William Wallace). London: Palgrave Macmillan, 21–37.

Han, Clara. 2013. "A long-term occupation: Police and the figures of the stranger." *Social Anthropology* 21.3: 378–84.

Han, Clara. 2020. *Seeing like a child: Inheriting the Korean War.* New York: Fordham University Press.

Han, Clara, and Andrew Brandel. 2020. "Genres of witnessing: Narrative, violence, generations." *Ethnos* 85.4: 629–46.

Heath-Kelly, Charlotte. 2013 "Counter-terrorism and the counterfactual: Producing the 'radicalisation' discourse and the UK PREVENT strategy." *The British Journal of Politics and International Relations* 15.3: 394–415.

Hiltebeitel, Alf. 1974. "Dumézil and Indian studies." *The Journal of Asian Studies* 34.1: 129–37.

Hinton, A. 1998. "Genocidal bricolage: A reading of liver-eating in Cambodia." Yale University Genocide Studies Program Working Paper GS 06: 16–38.

Humphrey, Caroline. 2021. "Corruption." In *Words and worlds: A lexicon for dark times* (eds. Veena Das and Didier Fassin). Durham, NC: Duke University Press, 185–204.

Jauregui, Beatrice. 2017. "Personal policing, ethnographic kinship, and critical empathy (India)." In *Writing the world of policing: The difference ethnography makes* (ed. Didier Fassin). Chicago, IL: University of Chicago Press, 62–90.

Kahn, Paul W. 2011. *Political theology: Four new chapters on the concept of sovereignty*. New York: Columbia University Press.

Kalyvas, Stathis N. 2006. *The logic of violence in civil war*. Cambridge: Cambridge University Press.

Kang, Han. 2017. *Human acts: A novel* (tr. Deborah Smith). London: Hogarth.

Kelly, Tobias. 2011. *This side of silence: Human rights, torture, and the recognition of cruelty*. Philadelphia: University of Pennsylvania Press.

Kennedy, David. 2006. *Of war and law*. Princeton, NJ: Princeton University Press.

Khan, Mahvish. 2008. *My Guantánamo diary: The detainees and the stories they told me*. Philadelphia, PA: Public Affairs.

Khan, Mohammad Aamir, and Nandita Haksar. 2016. *Framed as a terrorist: My 14-year struggle to prove my innocence*. New Delhi: Speaking Tiger Publishing.

Khoury, Elias. 2015. *Yalo* (tr. Peter Theroux). New York: Penguin Random House.

King, Michael, and Donald M. Taylor. 2011. "The

radicalization of homegrown jihadists: A review of theoretical models and social psychological evidence." *Terrorism and Political Violence* 23.4: 602–22.

Kublitz, Anja. 2021. "Omar is dead: Aphasia and the escalating anti-radicalization business." *History and Anthropology* 32.1: 64–77.

Kwon, Heonik. 2006. *After the massacre: Commemoration and consolation in Ha My and My Lai.* Berkeley: University of California Press.

Kwon, Heonik. 2008. *Ghosts of war in Vietnam.* Cambridge: Cambridge University Press.

Latour, Bruno. 2010. *The making of law: An ethnography of the Conseil d'Etat.* London: Polity.

Laugier, Sandra. 2015. "The ethics of care as a politics of the ordinary." *New Literary History* 46.2: 217–40.

Laugier, Sandra. 2018. "The vulnerability of reality: Austin, normativity, and excuses." In *Interpreting J.L. Austin: Critical Essays* (ed. Savas L. Tsohatzidis). Cambridge: Cambridge University Press, 119–42.

Laugier, Sandra. 2020. "Encounters of the third kind: Performative utterances and forms of life." *Inquiry*: 1–21. https://doi.org/10.1080/0020174X.2020.1784785.

Lawson, James. 2011. "Chronotope, story, and historical geography: Mikhail Bakhtin and the space-time of narratives." *Antipode* 43.2: 384–412.

Lazreg, Marnia. 2008. *Torture and the twilight of empire: From Algiers to Baghdad.* Princeton, NJ: Princeton University Press.

Lemaitre, Julieta. 2021. "War." In *Words and worlds: A lexicon for dark times* (eds. Veena Das and Didier Fassin). Durham, NC: Duke University Press, 143–65.

Levinson, Sanford. 2002. "Precommitment and postcommitment: The ban on torture in the wake of September 11." *Texas Law Review* 81: 2013–54.

Lokaneeta, Jinee. 2011. *Transnational torture.* New York: New York University Press.

Lokaneeta, Jinee. 2020. *The truth machines: Policing, vio-*

lence, and scientific interrogations in India. Ann Arbor: University of Michigan Press.

Manto, Saadat Hasan. 2008. *Selected stories*. London: Penguin Global.

Maunaguru, Sidharthan. 2020. "Vulnerable sovereignty: Sovereign deities and Tigers' politics in Sri Lanka." *Current Anthropology* 61.6: 686–712.

McDowell, John. 2008. "Comment on Stanley Cavell's 'Companionable thinking'." In *Philosophy and animal life* (Stanley Cavell, Cora Diamond, John McDowell, Ian Hacking & Cary Wolfe). New York: Columbia University Press, 127–38.

Mehta, Deepak. 2012. "Words that wound: Archiving hate in the making of Hindu-Indian and Muslim-Pakistani publics in Bombay." In *Beyond crisis* (ed. Naveeda Khan). New Delhi: Routledge India, 337–65.

Mehta, Deepak. 2015. "The Ayodhya dispute: The absent mosque, state of emergency and the jural deity." *Journal of Material Culture* 20.4: 397–414.

Mehta, Deepak. 2018. "The Ayodhya dispute: Law's imagination and the functions of the status quo." In *Violence and the quest for justice in South Asia* (eds. Deepak Mehta and Rahul Roy). Delhi: Sage Publications.

Mitchell, Oliver R. 1893. "The fictions of the law: Have they proved useful or detrimental to its growth?" *Harvard Law Review* VII.5: 249–65.

Moore, Nathan. 2012. "The perception of the middle." In *Deleuze and Law* (eds. Laurent Sutter and Kyle McGee). Edinburgh: Edinburgh University Press, 132–50.

Motta, Marco. 2019. "Ordinary realism: A difficulty for anthropology." *Anthropological Theory* 19.3: 341–61.

Motta, Marco. 2020. "The silent wars of the ordinary: Bitter neighborliness and the judiciary in Haiti." *The Journal of Legal Pluralism and Unofficial Law* 52.2: 111–33.

Mulla, Sameena. 2014. *The violence of care: Rape victims,*

forensic nurses, and sexual assault intervention. New York: NYU Press.

Ortner, Sherry B. 2016. "Dark anthropology and its others: Theory since the eighties." *HAU: Journal of Ethnographic Theory* 6.1: 47–73.

Osanloo, Arzoo. 2020. *Forgiveness work: Mercy, law, and victims' rights in Iran.* Princeton, NJ: Princeton University Press.

Peirce, Charles S. 1955. "Logic as semiotic: The theory of signs." In *Philosophical Writings of Peirce* (ed. Justus Buchler). New York: Dover Publications, 98–119.

Polloczek, Dieter Paul. 1999. "Utilitarian conscience and legal fictions in Bentham." *Angelaki: Journal of the Theoretical Humanities* 4.1: 81–98.

Punathil, Salah. 2020. "Archival ethnography and ethnography of archiving: Towards an anthropology of riot inquiry commission reports in postcolonial India." *History and Anthropology*: 1–19. https://doi.org/10.1080/02757206.2020.1854750.

Qureshi, Bilal. 2018. "The war for nostalgia: Sanjay Leela Bhansali's Padmaavat." *Film Quarterly* 71.4: 46–51.

Ralph, Laurence. 2020. *The torture letters: Reckoning with police violence.* Chicago, IL: University of Chicago Press.

Raman, Bhavani. 2017. "Law in times of counter-insurgency." In *Iterations of Law: Legal histories from India* (eds. Aparna Balachandran, Rashmi Pant, and Bhavni Raman). New Delhi: Oxford University Press, 120–46.

Rao, M. S. 2006. Keynote address given to the 93rd Indian science congress. http://mindjustice.org/india2-06.htm

Rao, Ursula. 2013. "Tolerated encroachment: Resettlement policies and the negotiation of the licit/illicit divide in an Indian metropolis." *Cultural Anthropology* 28.4: 760–79.

Rao, Vyjayanthi. 2006. "Slum as theory: The South /Asian city and globalization." *International Journal of Urban and Regional Research* 30.1: 225–32.

Rao, Vyjayanthi. 2007. "How to read a bomb: Scenes from Bombay's Black Friday." *Public Culture* 19.3: 567–92.

Rechtman, Richard. 2020. *La vie ordinaire de génocidaires*. Paris: CNRS Éditions.

Rechtman, Richard. 2021. *Living in death: Genocide and its functionaries* (tr. Lindsay Turner). New York: Fordham University Press.

Rejali, Darius. 2007. *Torture and democracy*. Princeton, NJ: Princeton University Press.

Robbins, Joel. 2013. "Beyond the suffering subject: Toward an anthropology of the good." *Journal of the Royal Anthropological Institute* 19.3: 447–62.

Robbins, Joel. 2016. "What is the matter with transcendence? On the place of religion in the new anthropology of ethics." *Journal of the Royal Anthropological Institute* 22.4: 767–81.

Rojas-Perez, Isaias. 2017. *Mourning remains: State atrocity, exhumations, and governing the disappeared in Peru's postwar Andes*. Stanford, CA: Stanford University Press.

Ross, Fiona. 2003. *Bearing witness: Women and the Truth and Reconciliation Commission in South Africa*. London: Sterling Press.

Roy, Ananya. 2011. "Slumdog cities: Rethinking subaltern urbanism." *International Journal of Urban and Regional Research* 35.2: 223–38.

Samuel, Geoffrey. 2015. "Is law a fiction?" In *Legal fictions in theory and practice* (eds. Maksymilian Del Mar and William Twining). New York: Springer, 31–54.

Satyogi, Pooja. 2019. "Law, police and 'domestic cruelty': Assembling written complaints from oral narratives." *Contributions to Indian Sociology* 53.1: 46–71.

Schmitt, Carl. 2005. *Political theology: Four chapters on the concept of sovereignty*. Chicago, IL: University of Chicago Press.

Schuurman, Bart. 2010. "Clausewitz and the 'new wars'

scholars." *The US Army War College Quarterly: Parameters* 40.1: 89–100.

Segal, Lotte Buch. 2018. "Tattered textures of kinship: The effects of torture among Iraqi families in Denmark." *Medical Anthropology* 37.7: 553–67.

Segal, Lotte Buch. 2020. "Torture and the veil of singularity: A commentary on Veena Das' 'Where is democracy in India? Asking anthropological theory to open its doors'." Anthropological Theory Commons blogpost. Available at: https://www.at-commons.com/2020/07/15/torture-and-the-veil-of-singularity-a-commentary-on-veena-das-where-is-democracy-in-india-asking-anthropological-theory-to-open-its-doors/.

Sehdev, Megha Sharma. 2018. *Interim artifacts of law: Interruption and absorption in Indian domestic violence cases.* Unpublished dissertation, Johns Hopkins University.

Shaikh, Abdul Wahid. 2017. *Begunah Qaidi: Atankvad ke Jhuthe Mukkadamon mein Phasaye Gaye Muslim Naujavanon ki Dastan [The innocent prisoner: Story of Muslim youth trapped in false cases of terrorism].* New Delhi: Pharos Media.

Simmel, Georg. 1965 [1906/1908]. "The poor." *Social Problems* 13.2: 118–40.

Simone, AbdouMaliq. 2004. "People as infrastructure: Intersecting fragments in Johannesburg." *Public Culture* 16.3: 407–29.

Simone, AbdouMaliq. 2019. *Improvised lives: Rhythms of endurance in an urban south.* Cambridge: Polity.

Simpson, Zacharia. 2012. "The truths we tell ourselves: Foucault on parrhesia." *Foucault Studies* 13: 99–115.

Singh, Bhrigupati. 2012. "The headless horseman of Central India: Sovereignty at varying thresholds of life." *Cultural Anthropology* 27.2: 383–407.

Singh, Bhrigupati. 2015. *Poverty and the quest for life: Spiritual and material striving in rural India.* Chicago, IL: University of Chicago Press.

Singh, Ujjwal Kumar. 2006. "The silent erosion: Anti-terror laws and shifting contours of jurisprudence in India." *Diogenes* 53.4: 116–33.

Singh, Ujjwal Kumar. 2007. *The state, democracy and anti-terror laws in India*. Delhi: Sage Publications.

Slahi, Mohamedou Ould. 2015. *Guantánamo diary* (ed. Larry Siems). New York: Little, Brown.

Spencer, Jonathan, ed. 2002. *Sri Lanka: History and the roots of conflict*. London: Routledge.

Steinberg, Jonah. 2019. *A garland of bones: Child runaways in India*. New Haven, CT: Yale University Press.

Stoler, Ann Laura. 2010. *Along the archival grain: Epistemic anxieties and colonial common sense*. Princeton, NJ: Princeton University Press.

Subbaraman, Ramnath, Laura Nolan, Kiran Sawant, et al. 2015. "Multidimensional measurement of household water poverty in a Mumbai slum: Looking beyond water quality." *PLOS One* 10.7: e0133241.

Suresh, Mayur. 2016. "The file as hypertext." In *Law, memory, violence: Uncovering the counter-archive* (ed. Stewart Motha and Honni van Rijswijk). London: Routledge, 97–115.

Suresh, Mayur. 2019. "The 'paper case': Evidence and narrative of a terrorism trial in Delhi." *Law & Society Review* 53.1: 173–201.

Talebi, Shahla. 2011. *Ghosts of revolution: Rekindled memories of imprisonment in Iran*. Stanford, CA: Stanford University Press.

Tarlo, Emma. 2003. *Unsettling memories: Narratives of the emergency in Delhi*. Berkeley: University of California Press.

Taylor, Chloë. 2009. *The culture of confession from Augustine to Foucault*. New York: Routledge.

Taylor, G. Flint. 2014. "The Chicago police torture scandal: A legal and political history." *CUNY Law Review* 17: 329–81.

Thénault, Sylvie. 2001. *Une drôle de justice: Les magistrats dans la guerre d'Algérie*. Paris: La Découvert.

Thomas, Yan, Marie-Angèle Hermitte, and Paolo Napoli. 2011. *Les opérations du droit*. Paris: EHESS.

Torre, María Elena, Michelle Fine, Kathy Boudin, et al. 2001. "A space for co-constructing counter stories under surveillance." New York: CUNY Academic Works, CUNY Graduate Center.

Tyagi, Shalini. 2019. "Importance of narco analysis test in investigation and its admissibility." *Journal of Legal Studies and Research* 3.1: 77–95.

Verdery, Katherine. 2018. *My life as a spy: Investigations in a secret police file*. Durham, NC: Duke University Press.

Vismann, Cornelia. 2008. *Files: Law and media technology* (tr. Geoffrey Winthrop-Young). Stanford, CA: Stanford University Press.

Walzer, Michael. 1973. "Political action: The problem of dirty hands." *Philosophy & Public Affairs* 2.2: 160–80.

Whitehead, Neil L. 2012. "Ethnography, silence, torture and knowledge." *History and Anthropology* 23.2: 271–82.

Wisnewski, J. Jeremy. 2008. "Unwarranted torture warrants: A critique of the Dershowitz proposal." *Journal of Social Philosophy* 39.2: 308–21.

Wolfendale, Jessica. 2009. "The myth of 'torture lite'." *Ethics & International Affairs* 23.1: 47–61.

Woloch, Alex. 2009. *The one vs. the many: Minor characters and the space of the protagonist in the novel*. Princeton, NJ: Princeton University Press.

Index

Index

Human Rights Commission 78

Ibrahim Dawood 38
Indian Evidence Act 49
Indra 15, 16–18, 72, 150n6, 151n8
  see also sovereignty
informal/unplanned settlements 73, 88–9, 149n1
informers *see* police informers
inhumanity 32–3, 63, 68, 95, 104–5
inordinate knowledge 109–10, 134, 147
  catastrophic events 34–70
  Cavell and 20–4, 35–6, 159n7
  circle of figures 21, 152n9
  difficulty of reality/difficulty of philosophy 20, 21–7, 35
  everyday life 44, 115, 147
  experience of/enduring 28, 35–6, 70, 128, 130
  meaning of 115
Institute for Socio-Economic Research on Development and Democracy (ISERDD) 103, 116, 158n3
interrogation 52, 59, 61–2
  enhanced interrogation techniques (EITs) 146, 161n5, 163n9
  routine questioning 61, 154n9
Islam *see* Muslims

jaankar (knowledgeable person) 83, 97
Jaffna 18–19
Jammu 144, 160n13
Jayasi, Mallik Mohammad 118

Jodha Akbar (film) 118
judicial truth 42–3, 72, 73
  see also legal fictions
July 11, 2006 bomb blasts 30, 49, 55
just war theory 8–9

Kang Kek Iew (Duch) 112
Kant, Immanuel 27, 160n14
Karni Sena 117, 122
Kashmir 128, 144, 160n13
Kaurava 18, 126, 151n7
Kelly, Tobias 154n8
Kh 87, 102–3, 112–13, 128–30, 140, 162n7
  court case 73, 76–82, 98–9
  stories 103–4, 129
Khmer Rouge regime 109, 110, 111–12, 159n8
kinship 32, 94–5
knowledgeable person (*jaankar*) 83, 97

labour 5, 73, 111n2
  see also work
land mafia (*bhu* mafia) 83, 88
language
  in confessions 72, 75–6
  context and 75
  courts 75–6
  documents 72, 75
  everyday life 63, 75–6, 126
  forms of life and 21, 65, 75
  Hindu–Muslim relations 124
  Sanskrit words 72, 75
  standing language 139, 162n8
Laugier, Sandra 36, 75, 124
law *see* courts, legal fictions, judicial truth, terror laws
legal fictions 3, 29–30, 32, 97–9